Straight from the Stacks

A Firsthand Guide to Careers in Library and Information Science

Laura Townsend Kane

American Library Association
Chicago 2003

While extensive effort has gone into ensuring the reliability of information appearing in this book, the publisher makes no warranty, express or implied, on the accuracy or reliability of the information, and does not assume and hereby disclaims any liability to any person for any loss or damage caused by errors or omissions in this publication.

Composition and design by ALA Editions in Optima and Sabon using QuarkXPress 5.0 for the PC

Printed on 50-pound white offset, a pH-neutral stock, and bound in 10-point coated cover stock by McNaughton & Gunn

The paper used in this publication meets the minimum requirements of American National Standard for Information Sciences—Permanence of Paper for Printed Library Materials, ANSI Z39.48-1992. ∞

Library of Congress Cataloging-in-Publication Data

Kane, Laura Townsend
    Straight from the stacks : a firsthand guide to careers in library and information science / Laura Townsend Kane.
        p. cm.
    Includes bibliographical references
    ISBN 0-8389-0865-9 (alk. paper)
    1. Library science—Vocational guidance—United States. 2. Information science—Vocational guidance—United States. 3. Librarians—Employment—United States. 4. Librarians—Job descriptions—United States. 5. Librarians—United States—Interviews. I. Title.
    Z682.35.V62K36 2004
    020′.23′73—dc21   2003012800

Printed in the United States of America

07   06   05   04   03   5   4   3   2   1

CONTENTS

ACKNOWLEDGMENTS

I would like to extend my gratitude to all who have helped to make this project a reality. In particular, a heartfelt "thank you" to each of the generous librarians featured in this book. They were a joy to work with, and their enthusiasm and cooperation made everything worthwhile! Thanks also to my co-workers, to my friends, and—most important—to my family for all their love and support throughout the completion of this endeavor.

INTRODUCTION

Early in my career as a professional librarian, a well-educated person said to me with disbelief, "You're a librarian? And you have to get a *master's* degree for that?" I was appalled. At around the same time, a co-worker of mine was speaking to an acquaintance at a party and mentioned that she worked as a cataloger in a library. "Well," the man replied wryly, "I suppose *someone* has to do it." That was ten years ago. Thankfully, the historically stereotypical image of librarianship has changed for the better, and people now recognize the importance of well-trained librarians in this technology-driven era. Still, we hear worrisome predictions about the future of our profession. In a few years' time, the bulk of the workforce will have retired and there will not be enough librarians to fill the vacant positions. To make matters worse, those positions will be high-level ones, and libraries will be left without well-trained leaders. Why is this? Librarianship is an exciting and versatile career; those working in the field today are taking an active part in shaping the Information Age. Why, then, are there not more students clamoring to earn advanced degrees in library and information science?

Looking back, I have to be honest with myself and admit that, if it hadn't been for luck and circumstance, I myself would not be a librarian today. I set out to be a Spanish teacher, and it was only when I started taking education courses that I realized teaching was not for me. At the time I was working as an assistant at the Augusta Technical Institute Library in Augusta, Georgia. A friend of mine who also worked there decided to pursue a graduate degree in library science. Despite the fact that I had volunteered or worked in libraries since elementary school, the idea of becoming a professional librarian never occurred to me. I spoke at length with my friend about her decision, and in a few months' time I decided to follow in her footsteps. I moved to Columbia, South Carolina, and earned my master's degree in library and information science from the University of South Carolina.

I realize now that the reason librarianship was not my initial career choice was simply because I did not know enough about the profession for it to be a viable choice. Despite being a prime candidate for the profession, no person or organization ever approached me to explain the merits of librarianship. This, I think, is one reason why there are not more people choosing the career. It is also one of the primary reasons I decided to write this book. People need to be made aware of the wonderful opportunities available to those with advanced degrees in library and information science. Though we are information specialists, many of us aren't so great at distributing information about and promoting our own profession.

The second purpose for writing this book was to help those already in the field make informed career choices. I am a cataloger at an academic health sciences library, but once again I did not consciously choose this path of librarianship but rather stumbled upon it. In library school I was unsure whether I wanted to work in a school library, a public library, or an academic library. I didn't know if I wanted to work in public services or technical services. Luck made the decision for me. To help pay tuition, I worked as a graduate assistant at the USC School of Medicine Library, and was offered a job there as head of Cataloging and Acquisitions soon after graduating. I have been in that position ever since. I love my job, but after ten years I sometimes wonder, "What else is out there? What career choices can I make as a librarian? Are there opportunities I'm not aware of?" I felt the need for a source that would provide an overview of all the different career choices available to those in my field. I wanted to learn firsthand what others with library degrees have accomplished throughout their careers. Such a source was not available, so I set about making one.

What an amazing process it turned out to be! I learned so much, but the number one revelation that remains with me is that librarianship is, first and foremost, a helping profession. Before I began, I worried about how to find people willing to talk about their jobs and their careers. It turns out I needn't have worried. After using the Internet to locate the names of librarians working in various positions, I nervously bit the bullet and started making calls and sending e-mail queries. I was overwhelmed at the response. Not only were these librarians willing to share a bit of themselves with me, they were eager to do so! Some even considered it an honor.

This project has served to renew my pride in being a librarian. Though the librarians featured in this book have jobs and backgrounds that are unique and diverse, they are all bound together by a common thread.

Many might say this commonality is information, but that is not quite accurate. It is a spirit of generosity that links them all together and serves as the backbone of our profession.

CHAPTER 1

Public Librarianship

There are only a few places in a community where every population group—regardless of age, race, ethnicity, or social status—is made to feel welcome. The public library is one of those places. Whether young, old, rich, poor, disabled, or homeless, every person who enters a public library can be confident that he or she will receive prompt, efficient, and unbiased service.

The cornerstone of public librarianship, then, is service. Most people who enter this field are driven by both an altruistic desire to help others and a deep-rooted fascination with technology and information. For those who are willing to serve all age groups, handle all types of requests for information, wear many hats for their job responsibilities, and work as a team player, public librarianship can be a richly rewarding career.

A handful of people these days still harbor the notion that public librarians spend their days sitting at desks reading books or checking out books to people. This is so far from the truth it is almost comical. Serving the information needs of a community is no small feat, and public librarians must possess administrative, managerial, and organizational skills in order to be successful. They must also be committed to continuing education, particularly in relation to changes in technology and developments in the provision of information. Specific responsibilities vary drastically among professional positions. Librarians within the public services arena are generally assigned titles such as reference librarian, circulation librarian, access services librarian, computer services librarian, and children's

1

services librarian. In technical services, job titles include catalog librarian, acquisitions librarian, serials librarian, and web management librarian.

Despite varied responsibilities and skills, all public librarians are linked together by a common commitment: equal information access for all. Knowledge is power, and public librarians provide empowerment to all citizens through equal access to information. This empowerment is the goal of the countless programs and services offered by public libraries. The quality of such programs and services is largely dependent upon a library's budget, which originates from public funding and private donations.[1] A large, well-funded library might offer a wide variety of programs for all age groups, while a smaller, less wealthy library might focus on only a few quality programs. This is why public librarians must work with public officials, trustees, and community leaders to seek the funding required for an active, robust community library. In addition to acquiring adequate funding, public librarians must study the community to learn the informational needs of its citizens and to discover the most appropriate ways to meet those needs.

A large percentage of Americans visit the nearly nine thousand public libraries in the United States at least once a year.[2] Studies have revealed that citizens consider their public library a source of educational and cultural enrichment as well as a source for entertainment. People utilize public library services to improve reading skills, to achieve success in school, to learn how to be more productive at work, and even to help overcome loneliness.[3] With such far-reaching influences, the public library is clearly a valuable and essential institution within each community. To be a public librarian is to be committed to the goals of that institution, to be dedicated to the delivery of information, and to embrace every person's right to access the collective knowledge of the past and the present, and the promised knowledge of the future.

SPOTLIGHTS

JOHN JOHNSON
Head of Reference Services
Keene Public Library
Keene, N.H.

John Johnson

"Being a reference librarian is hard-core public service," says John Johnson. "People skills and a willingness to work with the public are essential. If people aren't comfortable talking to you, you will never be able to draw them out enough to really answer a difficult question. You have to like people and be willing to deal with them on an extended basis in order to perform your job effectively."

As the head of Reference Services at Keene Public Library in Keene, New Hampshire, Johnson is responsible for maintaining the reference collection and for staffing the reference desk sixty-five hours per week. He and several other librarians work together to provide reference services to a variety of patron groups. "It is impossible to narrow down one group as our primary set of patrons," he says. "Our patrons range from families with infants to senior citizens. We are close to the local middle school and have a large group of preteens and teens every afternoon. Keene also has a state college, Keene State, and a lot of their students take advantage of the reciprocal borrowing agreement we have between us. There are also a couple of shelters within walking distance to the library with which we have made borrowing arrangements. In addition, we have numerous users who do not reside in the city of Keene but travel to the city to avail themselves of our services."

Johnson spends between three and five hours each day on the reference desk. Much of that time is spent answering questions, assisting patrons with the library's computers, signing people up to use the Internet, and requesting books for patrons through interlibrary loan. When he is not staffing the reference desk, he spends his time maintaining the reference collection. This includes selecting books for purchase, completing regular inventories, and weeding the collection. In addition, he teaches three weekly training sessions on basic computer use.

"Being a reference librarian means that you are one of the most visible representatives of the entire library," says Johnson. "Your attitude toward the public is the attitude library patrons perceive as belonging to the whole staff. You have to be ready to switch mental gears depending on what each patron is looking for. Again, the most essential skills are your people skills."

Johnson finds that the most rewarding part of his job is being able to help people locate the information they need. "I really enjoy trying to track down information for a patron," he says. "When someone comes in with a question, that makes my time at the desk enjoyable." He also enjoys watching people continue to learn on their own after he has given them some initial computer training. "I had one student, a gentleman in his 70s, who came in to learn how to use a computer and e-mail. He is now a regular on our Internet computers. He happily let us know that when he went on vacation he was able to keep up with his e-mail by visiting the local library where he was staying. He is now active in a chat room that has been set up by the alumni foundation of his alma mater."

"The thing I like least about my job is having to try to control the middle school and high school kids who come into the library after school," Johnson says. "Unfortunately, these kids are basically left at the library from the time school gets out until their parents get off work at night. Their natural rambunctiousness, while understandable, is not acceptable in a library."

Librarianship was not an initial career goal for Johnson. "In fact," he says, "I drifted into working in libraries." After receiving a B.S. in computer science from Clarkson University, he went back to school part-time to get a B.A. in mathematics at SUNY Plattsburgh. To help pay tuition, he took a job as a page at the Plattsburgh Public Library. Deciding that he enjoyed working in libraries, Johnson took another position as the evening circulation supervisor at the SUNY Plattsburgh Library. He completed his B.A. and went on to earn his library degree through the distance education program at Syracuse University.

After graduation, Johnson moved to Arizona and became the outreach librarian for the Mohave County Library District. "As outreach librarian I was primarily responsible for supporting the eight smaller libraries scattered throughout Mohave County. After a couple of years in that position, I was promoted to Worksystems manager for the district. Worksystems was intended to study how the library operated and improve efficiency wherever possible. After being in the desert for three and a half years, I wanted to return to the greenery of the northeast. I was lucky to get the job here at the Keene Public Library as head of Reference Services."

With his background in computer science, Johnson is able to adapt to new technology with ease. "I enjoy playing with the new 'toys' the library gets," he says. "Every time we get new equipment or subscribe to a new database, I play around with it until I've figured out how to use it. I still try to keep up with my reading on the direction technology is heading, though I'm not as diligent with it as I should be." Johnson also subscribes to several electronic discussion groups to maintain contact with colleagues and to keep up with new types of technologies used by other libraries. He pursues a wide variety of training and has recently attended workshops on digital collections, ethics, and safety. He belongs to the American Library Association and the New Hampshire Library Association and takes advantage of training opportunities offered by various state and regional library associations.

Johnson says that to be an effective reference librarian in a public library, people skills are absolutely essential. "If you can't interact with the public, you can't help them," he explains. "It also helps to enjoy the search for information. If you don't enjoy looking up obscure bits of information, you won't have any satisfaction with your work. Adaptability is another essential skill. Libraries are always changing. You must be able to change and keep up with what is going on around you."

Johnson recommends taking all the reference and database-searching classes offered in library school. "It doesn't matter if you're being trained on a database that 99 percent of public libraries in the country can't afford. The experience of using it will translate into whatever you will be using when you get your first library job." Since most librarians today are given multiple responsibilities, Johnson recommends taking management courses as well. "Slowly fading are the days when you could just be a reference librarian," he says. "These days, professional librarians are expected to take part in the management of a library."

"The hardest part of getting a job as a reference librarian is getting your foot in the door," Johnson says. "Once you have experience, you can find jobs. It often helps to have worked in libraries as a paraprofessional before getting your degree, because some libraries are willing to accept this as required work experience."

To Johnson, being a librarian in this new millennium means being adaptable to new technologies and being able to maintain the skills needed to answer questions and to match readers with books. "The basic core of librarianship remains the same," he says. "The mindset of service and getting the patron[s] what they need hasn't changed. It is the tools we use to perform our basic functions that are in a constant state of change. Librarians will have to become more adaptable in order to keep up with the accelerating rate of change we all face in the workplace."

KAREN TOBIN
Head of Circulation/Assistant Director
Marlborough Public Library
Marlborough, Mass.

"I have always wanted to work in public libraries. I believe that they touch people's lives and change them for the better in ways that no other library can." At the Marlborough Public Library in Marlborough, Massachusetts, Karen Tobin has the opportunity to touch people's lives

Karen Tobin

on a constant basis. As head of circulation and assistant director, her job requires direct interaction with both the library staff and the general public. Just as people are unpredictable, so is Tobin's job. Most challenging—and exciting—to her is the fact that she never knows exactly what she might be required to face on any given day.

"My role is jack-of-all-trades," says Tobin. "I train, schedule, and supervise circulation staff. This comprises about twenty people, including part-timers and pages. I am also the de facto technology specialist in our library and am responsible for in-house maintenance, installation, and deployment of computers." Her routine varies from day to day, depending on what challenges await her upon entering the library each morning. When staff members are absent, she must make arrangements to ensure that the circulation desk is staffed throughout the day. When computer issues arise, it falls upon her to handle them. She has participated in several major computer upgrades and installations, including the development of a request for proposal (RFP), the selection of equipment, and the design of the library's physical computer configuration. Tobin also serves on the Space Needs/Building Committee, which is in the early stages of looking into a new library facility. Finally, she serves several hours a week on both the circulation and reference desks, participates in the library's budget process, and acts in a leadership capacity in the director's absence.

"Our clientele is varied, as it is in so many public libraries," Tobin says. "We serve everyone from babies to senior citizens. The community has shifted in recent years from predominantly blue-collar to white-collar, so the median education level has risen accordingly. In addition, we have a fairly large immigrant population, so we obtained a grant to start collecting in other languages, particularly Brazilian Portuguese and Spanish in order to serve that segment of the community."

Librarianship, for Tobin, is a calling. "I was born this way," she says. She has been working in the Marlborough Public Library since serving as a page during high school. Throughout college, she would return to work there during the summers. Shortly after graduating with her bachelor's degree, she accepted a full-time circulation position at the library. She was subsequently promoted to government documents librarian and served in that position for twelve years. It was after being promoted to cataloger/head of Technical Services that Tobin enrolled in the University of Rhode Island and earned her library degree. Afterward, she moved into the head of circulation/assistant director position.

As an information professional, Tobin classifies her role as "conduit, trainer, and guide." Knowing the importance of keeping up with technology, she reads professional literature and subscribes to various electronic discussion groups. "I also take advantage of any training that is made available through our network or the regional library system," she adds. "I have taken commercial seminars in computers and administrative skills. I've also taken a course in Portuguese in order to communicate better with some of our newest patrons."

Tobin says that a successful circulation librarian in a public library must be willing to learn and to take on any task that needs to be done. "Also, you really need to like working with people, all kinds of people," she adds. "Patrons come to the library for so many different reasons, with so many different attitudes. Some are a joy to serve; some are not. But we need to serve them all. We need to help the person who doesn't really know how to ask for what he or she wants, as well as the person who asks confidently and commandingly." She advises becoming comfortable and conversant with computers and to develop the skills necessary to train others to use computers. "It's so much a part of what we do, and a good training experience makes a huge difference to patrons and staff."

For Tobin, being a librarian today means the same as it has for centuries past. "It's all about service, service, service," she says. "It's simple. We have the information. They want the information. We get it for them or teach them how to get it themselves. It's the same process, whether the information comes from the most sophisticated search engine or from *Webster's Dictionary*."

Christine Hendel

CHRISTINE HENDEL
Library Services Supervisor
Technical Services
Thousand Oaks Library System
Thousand Oaks, Calif.

In Thousand Oaks, California, the public library is a valued resource to a wide variety of people. The area, sometimes known as the "Technology Corridor," is the site of the world headquarters of a number of big-name corporations and agencies. Many employees of these corporations utilize the library as a source for high-tech business information. Located halfway between Los Angeles and Santa Barbara, the city also boasts growing Hispanic and Chinese communities, both of which are active library user groups. Effective customer service and delivery of information, whether to a toddler or to a businessperson, is the primary mission of the Thousand Oaks Library System. Librarian Chris Hendel plays a vital role in the success of this mission.

As library services supervisor in charge of Technical Services, Hendel is responsible for supervising the nineteen staff members who order, catalog, and process all library materials. "I am a facilitator," she says. "I ensure that new materials are purchased economically and that they are cataloged and processed quickly so that they are available when the public needs them." Hendel is also responsible for the integrity of bibliographic information in the library's online catalog. "Technical Services must make the information in the database representing library materials very accessible and easily understood and found," she explains. "My role is to ensure high-quality records production and adherence to consistent standards."

Hendel has recently been deeply involved in converting from one integrated library system to another. Since virtually all of the modules in the new system have to be mastered by the Technical Services staff, this project has had a major impact on her department. "Besides decision making, which is considerable, coordinating the training takes a remarkable amount of time," she says. "As the system is being implemented gradually, the Technical Services workflow and assignment of job functions have to be reevaluated and adjusted constantly. As we proceed through the various modules, procedure manual documents are being written and revised on a daily basis." After two years of preparation and the implementation of a number of modules, she feels that they have accomplished a lot but still have a long way to go.

In addition to serving as department manager and providing leadership to her staff, Hendel shares responsibility as building supervisor with other senior staff members. "When staff is unable to resolve issues with patrons, the building supervisor of the day will deal with the patron and make decisions," she says. "In the event of an emergency, I am responsible for ensuring proper actions are taken, such as evacuating the building or dealing with a medical crisis." As a senior librarian, she also serves on the Director's Advisory Council in which library policies and issues are discussed.

"Between memos, e-mail, and meetings, many of which are held in another building about seven miles away, I spend my time signing invoices and timesheets, reviewing incoming book and other materials orders, juggling staff based on workflow needs, and dealing with all those issues and questions that needed decisions yesterday," Hendel says. "I also manage the science fiction collection, including selection, weeding, mending, and sorting through donations." In addition, to keep up her reference skills, she makes an effort to help out at the reference desk from time to time.

Hendel finds enjoyment and excitement in the various aspects of her job. "As a detail-oriented person, I really enjoy simply working with the books," she says. "I like overseeing the functions of cataloging and acquisitions, and I help out when I can. This hands-on approach really helps in understanding what the staff is doing on a daily basis and often can lead to innovations or discovery of problems that otherwise might not come to light." She does find that her multiple responsibilities can be challenging at times. "Sometimes I think that there should be three people to do the work I have in order to accomplish it all. There's no nine-to-five in this job, and I know I am not the only senior supervisor to be found working late."

Despite constraints on her time, Hendel still manages to promote camaraderie and fun among the staff. She recently spearheaded the development of the library's "Cart Wheelers Precision Drill Team" for the Conejo Valley Days parade. Dozens of staff members, from pages to senior librarians, collaborated to design and produce costumes and carts for the parade. Serving as drill team leader and armed with a whistle and flash cards, Hendel designed multiple serpentine precision routines and led the practice many Friday evenings for three months. The staff threw themselves into the effort and learned to perform all kinds of intricate moves, marching to the beat of patriotic music. "Led by librarians holding a giant Thousand Oaks Library sign on poles, our procession won lots of applause, amazement, and laughter in our first parade last year," says Hendel. "I can't think of another event that was so effective in drawing our staff together in a collective off-duty effort. I was so proud of us all. It was such fun—a chance to laugh and to make others laugh too. What a wonderful way to remind our patrons of our commitment to the community!"

Hendel has worked in libraries for most of her life, beginning as a volunteer shelving books in junior high, working as a student aide in college, and going full-time upon graduation. "Yet," she says, "if you had asked me back then if I wanted to be a librarian, I would have scoffed at the idea." For many years she worked as a paraprofessional in various reference and technical services positions in different institutions. In between library jobs, she tried her hand at studying textile technology and even, at one point, opened her own needlework shop. After the new Thousand Oaks Library was built, she was hired in the Acquisitions unit and later became a senior library assistant in charge of Serials, where she had the opportunity to test the Acquisitions module of the library's integrated system and to implement the change from manual to automated procedures. "At that point," she says, "I could not progress any higher as a paraprofessional, and I needed to increase my income." She enrolled at San Jose State University's program at California State University, Fullerton, and earned her library science degree.

"I think going to library school was one of the best decisions I have ever made," says Hendel. "Even though I had already worked for ten years in libraries when I started library school, the classes completely changed my perspective and understanding of library issues." Since she was working in the Thousand Oaks Library Serials Unit while in library school, she was able to immediately implement her new skills. She took computer classes and learned to become proficient in word processing, spreadsheets, and database creation, all of which helped her with her job. Her management, cataloging, and reference classes were also particularly helpful in the "real world" of work.

Within three months of graduating she was promoted to reference librarian, and three months after that she was put in charge of implementing a grant that provided Internet access to the public. "This grant provided a great many wonderful classes and workshops, which eventually enabled me to create and maintain an extensive web page for the library. After over five years as webmaster, I was promoted to senior librarian in charge of Technical Services. It is a little ironic that I am now supervising the staff that supervised me nineteen years ago!"

Hendel is a member of the American Library Association, the Public Library Association, and the California Library Association. To keep up with changing technology, she attends conferences and reviews professional literature. She attends seminars, user group meetings, and other classes to update her management and technical skills.

As advice to those interested in technical services librarianship, Hendel recommends working in a technical services position for at least a year or, at the very least, completing a technical services internship. A thorough understanding of acquisitions, cataloging, and serials functions is necessary in order to be successful. For supervisory positions, Hendel feels that additional skills in management techniques are needed. "Dealing with staffing issues, scheduling, performance evaluations, and performance or behavior problems requires special sensitivity, communication skills, and experience," she explains. "It is worthwhile taking all the training courses available both before and after becoming a manager. Above all, maintain persistence, patience, poise, and a positive attitude! A commitment to excellence and an interest in seeing jobs well done have been a successful recipe for me."

Hendel welcomes the challenge of being a librarian in this technology-driven era. "In these days of the Internet and metadata and push technology, skilled librarians are needed more than ever," she says. "Studies have confirmed that the Internet has not replaced a need for librarians or libraries. In fact, some of the heaviest library users are Internet users. Librarians need to continue to constantly update their skills to be competitive, informed, and professional."

DANIEL C. HORNE
Consumer Health Librarian
New Hanover County Public Library
Wilmington, N.C.

Dan Horne knows firsthand what it is like to be in desperate need of quality health information for consumers. In 2002, he underwent a liver transplant. As a consumer health librarian in a public library, he was fortunate to have had the

Daniel C. Horne

background and the expertise required to locate precisely the information he needed. Though the experience was a difficult one for him, it helped to reinforce his conviction that every consumer undergoing a health crisis should be given access to authoritative health information through trained advocates within the public library system.

At the New Hanover Public Library in Wilmington, North Carolina, Horne's main responsibility is the management of the Consumer Health Library. He and his staff provide health reference information to the general public. "Most public reference librarians are generalists and must be ready to answer questions or find information on any topic put before them. However, some branches of reference require special knowledge," he says. "Those librarians who are active in the field of consumer health are specialists, and usually have had formal training in health-related subjects such as medical terminology, anatomy, and physiology."

Horne observes that some public reference librarians are anxious about medical reference. "Anxiety comes from uncertainty about the vocabulary and the fear of giving incorrect information, a fear made more acute because their answer may have an effect on a person's physical and mental well-being," he explains. His remedy is to always follow a certain set of rules regarding the provision of health-related information. Rule number one is to never diagnose or recommend procedures. "If you do," he says, "you will be practicing medicine without a license and may place yourself in legal jeopardy."

"Never give information off the top of your head," Horne continues. "Always look it up even if you are sure of the answer, and always cite your source. Never refer to or speak unfavorably about a particular practitioner or clinic. Instead, invite the patron to use your reference materials or those you've posted on the Internet. Finally, when you feel you have been presented with a request that is beyond your scope, do not hesitate to refer people back to their physician. With these rules in mind, always do whatever it takes to find people the information they need while maintaining a real attitude of support, concern, or sympathy."

In addition to helping the general public, Horne works closely with health professionals who provide outreach services. He acts as a coordinator between agencies such as the local medical center, the medical library, and the university library in providing quality consumer health information. "I try to make things easy for my clientele by providing information access through multiple avenues such as e-mail, voice mail, our website, and, of course, direct patron contact," he says.

"Public service is both the most challenging and exciting feature of my job," says Horne. "I love difficult reference, the kind that forces you to dive deep into all your resources and which taxes your library knowledge and skills. I also enjoy the challenge of providing medical reference for people of all ages seeking information on virtually all branches of health and medicine."

When he is not spending time in service to the public, Horne has various other duties related to the administration of the Consumer Health Library. He manages the budget allotted to the collection and is responsible for selecting books and periodicals for purchase. He is involved with collection maintenance, website development, upkeep of the vertical file, and committee work. "In the morning, I answer e-mails and telephone queries and complete leftover business from the previous day," he says. "When not helping patrons, I endeavor to work on my other responsibilities. Sometimes, when necessary, I work reference in the local history and genealogy section as well as youth services. I enjoy these assignments because I always learn something new to help keep my skills sharp." Due to meetings, projects, travel, vacations, and illness, Horne is aware that he cannot always be at the library. Hence, he takes measures to ensure that his staff is well trained in the provision of consumer health reference so service may continue in his absence.

Throughout his experience as a consumer health librarian, Horne has made many observations about patrons and about the specialty. "There is a middle area between the general descriptions of medical conditions found in consumer health sources and the technical material prepared for health professionals," he says. "Most people need information that lies within this middle area. Providing just the right information is challenging." He has also found that, while women are avid seekers of consumer health information, men don't generally seek such information on their own.

"Consumers do not entirely trust the medical establishment," Horne continues. "They are concerned about the quality of physicians and hospitals and resent the often offhand and sometimes even rude manner in which they are treated. Alternative therapies are popular because they offer people the chance to control their own treatments without the intervention of the medical establishment. Patrons often tell me about the importance of being one's own advocate in negotiating the maze of the health care system. They feel that if they don't take responsibility, no one else will."

According to surveys, consumers seek medical information to increase their knowledge of treatments and procedures and to reduce fear and anxiety about their conditions. Horne finds that, when confronted by potentially catastrophic health problems, people often convey a matter-of-fact attitude and display a sense of humor about their illness. When patrons do display emotion, it is usually over the condition of a loved one. "Patrons want us to give them advice," says Horne. "This is a great danger, and we must be very careful to phrase statements in such a way that what we are saying cannot in any way be considered advice."

Though born in Hawaii, Horne spent much of his life in the San Francisco Bay area of California. He earned a B.A. in English from UC Davis and went on to receive his library science degree from San Jose State University. Most of his professional experience has involved reference service in public library settings. He served as head of the Life Sciences Library at NASA's Ames Research Center in Mountain View, California. He has also worked as an outreach librarian, as the head of a technical services department, and even as manager of a bookmobile. After moving to North Carolina with his family in search of more affordable real estate, Horne took a job as head of Reference for the New Hanover County Public Library (NHCPL). "After ten years in that position, I left to start up a consumer health library at our medical center," he says. "This was the most fun I've ever had as a professional librarian. What librarian wouldn't take the opportunity to start up an entire library?" When financial difficulties forced the collection to be moved from the medical center to NHCPL, Horne returned there and accepted his current position. He is happy to report that NHCPL is currently undergoing renovations that include space for a new consumer health library.

Horne is a big believer in keeping up with technology. "Libraries and computer technology are made for each other. It is, therefore, important to have a solid working knowledge of the technology available to you at your library and also to be aware of general information technology trends and products." As advice on keeping up with technology and staying marketable as a librarian, Horne says, "Join an electronic discussion group and ask questions. Go to conferences, attend technology sessions, and visit vendor booths. Talk to colleagues to learn how they use technology and learn as much as you can about computers."

For those interested in becoming consumer health librarians, Horne says that career planning is very important. "If you know beforehand that you want to enter the field of consumer health, go to a library school that has a medical librarian program," he says. "Even when you apply for a position as a general reference librarian, any training in consumer health will help you. This could open for you a doorway to becoming a consumer health librarian." He recommends maintaining a membership in the

Medical Library Association (MLA) and its Consumer and Patient Health Information Section. Becoming certified in MLA's Consumer Health Information Specialization Program is also helpful.

"It doesn't hurt to get some formal training in consumer health–related subjects," he adds. "You can take courses at a local community college or health agency. Important, too, is self-training. Read your health and medicine newsletters. Watch consumer health videos. Read a good (but not too difficult) book about the human body. Keep track of new developments and terminology. Your employer may have software training available. Take what you need and immediately apply your new skill to your job."

Horne feels that the provision of consumer health information is a significant issue for public libraries today. "There is a growing realization that quality of life depends to a large extent on good health," he says. "Good health is no longer viewed as just the absence of disease. Proper nutrition and exercise, stress reduction, freedom from harmful habits and addictions, interior and exterior environmental health, and spiritual and emotional growth are now emphasized. Parents are concerned about the total health of their children. Young adults and members of the baby boom generation see health and fitness as vital to success in their careers and in family life. People who have reached the end of their careers know that retirement is more than just not having to go to work anymore; it is a time when dreams of travel and accomplishments can be realized. Grandparents want to be healthy so they can be a positive force in the lives of their grandchildren. As librarians, we know that one of the major keys to success in any endeavor is accurate and current information. Nowhere is this truer than in fighting disease and maintaining health. Good information is truly the best medicine!"

CINDY PAGE
Government Documents Librarian
Houston Public Library
Houston, Tex.

As the government documents librarian at Houston Public Library, Cindy Page is responsible for the management of the oldest and largest depository of government publications in the Houston area. Certain libraries throughout the

Cindy Page

country are designated as "depositories" for the numerous publications released by the United States government. While most libraries collect in only certain subject areas, Page's collection is large, comprehensive, and, in some areas, archival.

"I see my role as being an advocate for the Depository Library Program, the Government Printing Office, and government information in general, and being a conservator of the library's government publications collection," says Page. She is responsible for the daily operation of the depository collection. She supervises two library assistants whose duties are to process and retrieve materials and maintain the collection. She selects and deselects publications, gives orientations to the documents collection, and, as the liaison to the Government Printing Office (GPO), prepares such reports as biennial surveys and GPO inspections.

"The main difference between Government Documents and other areas of public librarianship," Page says, "is that I have to, in effect, serve two masters. I have to be aware of regulations and issues related to GPO and the depository program in order to be in compliance as a depository, but I have to fit those processes into the needs and goals of the Houston Public Library. It is up to me to make sure the library administration is aware of GPO requirements, and I have to balance those requirements with the library's capabilities."

Page's position falls within the library's Business/Science Technology department. Typically she spends a third of her time staffing the reference desk within that department. Though the reference desk is not actually in the documents area, the librarians frequently rely on government documents to answer questions. "Government documents show up in all catalog searches as though they were books on the shelf, so we tend to treat documents just like any other source," Page explains.

"As the central public library in the fourth largest city in America, we serve just about every type of patron you can imagine," she continues. "We help sixth graders with their science fair projects, M.B.A. students with their papers, homeless transients [with] the Internet, downtown business people with their need for statistics, and the nearby office worker who runs in on a lunch hour looking for a tax form. Any of our varied patrons could be directed to government sources if that is what it takes to answer the question. I find that, very often, people do not realize it is government information that they need."

Though she works with government documents every day, Page is still amazed when a particular document turns out to meet the exact information needs of a patron. "I think that some of the most gratifying times occur when you least expect to help someone with government information," she says. "Just recently a man came up to the desk and said that he wanted information about commercial fishing boats. This gentleman truthfully looked more like one of our homeless regulars than someone with a 'real' question." Page showed the man the circulating books about boats and ships, and then checked the online catalog. She found a document dealing with regulations produced by the Transportation Department and showed it to the patron. "He had not mentioned a word about needing regulations, but he came back about fifteen minutes later, grinning, and said that the document was exactly what he needed. Who would have guessed?"

In another instance, Page helped make a young student's day by finding an Army Technical Manual explaining how a tuba is constructed and how to take care of one. "We don't often deal with musical instrument questions in the Business Library," she says, "but this technical manual proved to be exactly what was needed. Again, who would have guessed?"

Some reference questions have raised interesting issues. A patron was looking for a report written in 1860 by a government civil servant, and though the library did not have the actual document, Page was able to find some solid leads for the patron to follow. "That someone who is interested in this report 140 years later and can reasonably expect to find it is pretty amazing," she says. "What is disconcerting is to think whether government employees' reports might be accessible 140 years from now. Who is going to save e-mails and disks, and how will they be available? We already have trouble accessing DOS-based floppies distributed only fifteen years ago. We have to keep older computers around just to read 1990 Census CDs."

Page has an undergraduate degree in history from North Texas State University (NTSU). Soon after receiving her B.A., she enrolled in NTSU's library school, where, in addition to the required classes, she elected to take a government publications course. After graduating with her library degree, she moved to Australia with her husband and found a position as a cataloger at a small public library in Campbelltown, New South Wales. Upon returning to the United States and moving to the Houston area, she found a job as a reference librarian in the Business/Science Technology department at the Houston Public Library. She later became the documents librarian and has been in the position ever since.

"It does not take any particular skills to work with government documents," says Page. "Anyone can be trained. I think that the most important thing is to have an interest in documents and to have some affinity for details. A lot of librarians are somewhat 'scared' of documents, feeling that it is an area full of mystery as well as technicality. I have always attempted to put librarians at ease when I give orientations, pointing out the diversity of types of information and publications that are government documents."

"Keeping up with the changing electronic environment is definitely the most challenging aspect of my job," continues Page. "Since a computer was something I only got to observe in library school, all of my knowledge and experience has been acquired on the job." Technology has changed many aspects of her job since she was initially hired. For years, the government documents were not cataloged, and reference librarians really had to "know their stuff" in order to help patrons. Then, in the 1990s, records for the documents were entered into the online catalog. "With document records in the catalog for the first time, the increase in our retrievals was phenomenal," Page says. "It was great! Now, several years into our online catalog, the usage of our paper documents collection is down again. 'Everything' is online, and no one wants to come to the library to use it!"

In the Houston area, government documents librarians from nine institutions meet regularly to discuss documents-related issues and to hear reports from various conferences. To keep up with these issues and to maintain contact with colleagues, Page attends these Depository Library conferences and Depository Council meetings whenever possible. She is also a member of the Texas Library Association.

"Librarians in general, and government documents librarians in particular, face a challenging future," concludes Page. "The whole issue of preserving government information is so huge. Fortunately, there are a lot of sharp people, librarians as well as GPO personnel and others, who recognize the importance of access to government information and are working toward solving those issues."

SAMPLE JOB DESCRIPTIONS

Reference Librarians

Environment

In public libraries, the reference librarian is responsible for providing reference service and readers' advisory service to patrons of all age groups. Those librarians with the job title "Head of Reference" are responsible for the overall management of the reference department. This encompasses the supervision of staff, scheduling of the reference desk, development of the reference collection, and participation in budget allocation. Many reference librarians are given responsibility for service in other departments such as Circulation, Interlibrary Loan, or Computer Services. All of these areas involve direct interaction with library patrons. The number of staff working in the reference department is dependent upon the library's size and budget.

Responsibilities

Provide reference and readers' advisory service to all patrons

Notice and approach individuals who may need reference help

Utilize all available resources (print, electronic, online, telephone, etc.) to answer reference questions for patrons

Choose sources appropriate to the questions asked and to the patrons' objectives and level of expertise

Suggest other support services when appropriate

Keep abreast of new resources as they are added to the library collection or as access has been provided

Instruct patrons in the use of the library's online catalog as well as other relevant databases

Supervise all staff assigned to the reference department

Oversee the staffing and scheduling of the reference desk

Participate in the maintenance of the reference collection (book and journal selection, weeding, budget allocation, etc.)

Establish policies and procedures for the department

Compile reference department statistics on a weekly, monthly, or yearly basis

Participate in periodic evaluation of employees

Assist in the promotion of library programs services

Participate in special projects as needed

Perform duties in other departments as needed

Education and Training

A master's degree in library and information science from an ALA-accredited institution is generally required. Previous experience or course work emphasizing reference or public service is recommended.

Recommended Memberships

American Library Association (ALA)

Public Library Association (PLA), a division of ALA

Regional and local library associations

Circulation Librarians

Environment

Circulation librarians in public libraries manage all functions of the circulation department and interact on a constant basis with library staff and with library patrons of all ages. Additional duties within other public services areas, such as interlibrary loan or reference, are often expected. Circulation departments vary in size but often consist of at least one librarian and a number of support staff members.

Responsibilities

Supervise all staff within the circulation department, including professional librarians, support staff, and student workers

Oversee the staffing and scheduling of the circulation desk

Establish circulation policies and procedures

Communicate policies to patrons and staff as necessary

Coordinate training of all circulation staff in the implementation of departmental policies and procedures

Manage the circulation subsystem of the library's online catalog

Oversee the enrollment of new patrons to the library

Supervise the receiving and recording of overdue fines

Oversee the return of books and materials to shelves or storage places

Compile circulation statistics on a weekly, monthly, or yearly basis

Participate in periodic evaluation of employees

Assist in the promotion of library programs and services

Participate in special projects as needed

Perform duties in other departments as needed

Education and Training

A master's degree in library and information science from an ALA-accredited institution is generally required. Previous experience or course work with an emphasis on reference or public service is recommended.

Recommended Memberships

American Library Association (ALA)

Public Library Association (PLA), a division of ALA

Regional and local library associations

Technical Services Librarians

Environment

Technical services librarians in public libraries are responsible for all the steps involved with the ordering, receiving, cataloging, and processing of books, journals, and other library materials. Often, the technical services duties in a large library are divided among librarians with distinct titles and training such as cataloging librarian, acquisitions librarian, and serials librarian. In smaller libraries, one or two librarians may be responsible for all technical services duties. Though historically these positions involve little direct contact with the public, it is becoming more common for librarians in technical services to be assigned reference or other public service duties.

Responsibilities

Supervise the verification, ordering, and receipt of books, journals, and other library materials

Establish policies and procedures for the department

Train employees in the use of acquisitions and cataloging software or systems

Manage the library's materials budget; oversee allocation of funds according to subject areas, departments, materials format, etc.

Interact with publishers and vendors on a regular basis

Keep abreast of issues regarding book and serial acquisition, particularly those concerning electronic formats

Prepare statistical or financial reports on a weekly, monthly, or yearly basis

Maintain use statistics of both print and electronic collections

Review gift materials and manage gift acknowledgments

Supervise the cataloging and physical processing of library materials

Manage the library's bibliographic online catalog

Maintain expert knowledge of cataloging utilities, standards, and rules

Participate in collection development

Participate in periodic evaluation of employees

Perform duties in other departments as needed

Education and Training

A master's degree in library and information science from an ALA-accredited institution is generally required. Experience or course work with emphasis on cataloging or technical services is recommended.

Recommended Memberships

American Library Association (ALA)

Public Library Association (PLA), a division of ALA

Association for Library Collections and Technical Services (ALCTS), a division of ALA

Regional and local library associations

Systems/Automation Librarians

Environment

Systems librarians in public libraries are responsible for the administration and overall maintenance of the library's integrated library system as well as any computer-related systems or equipment used by library staff or patrons. Systems librarians must interact with library staff as well as library patrons as the need arises. Generally, library systems departments consist of one or two librarians and a varied number of support staff members.

Responsibilities

Manage and troubleshoot the library's integrated library system, including all standard modules such as cataloging, circulation, serials check-in, OPAC, interlibrary loan, and system administration

Maintain, update, and troubleshoot all computer software and equipment

Provide desktop support to library patrons and staff

Perform system-wide upgrades as required

Supervise in-house database projects

Prepare and provide statistical and other reports on a weekly, monthly, or yearly basis

Stay abreast of emerging technologies as related to library systems, the Internet, computer equipment, software, etc.

Participate in library web page development

Establish policies and procedures for the department

Keep staff informed of any technological or equipment changes

Participate in periodic evaluation of employees

Education and Training

A master's degree in library and information science from an ALA-accredited institution is generally required. Experience or course work with emphasis on systems administration or computer technology is recommended.

Recommended Memberships

American Library Association (ALA)

Public Library Association (PLA), a division of ALA

Library and Information Technology Association (LITA)

Regional and local library associations

Notes

1. Librarians in the Twenty-First Century: Public Librarians, 2000, available at http://www.istweb.syr.edu/21stcenlib/who/public.html. Accessed 26 February 2003.
2. Public Librarianship—It's More than You Think, 2003, available at http://www.pla.org/projects/recruitment.html. Accessed 26 February 2003.
3. Bernard F. Vavrek, "Is the American Public Library Part of Everyone's Life?" *American Libraries* 31, no. 1 (Jan. 2000): 60–64.

CHAPTER 2

School Media Librarianship/ Child and Young Adult Librarianship

SCHOOL MEDIA LIBRARIANSHIP

The school library media profession offers many diverse career opportunities for individuals who are highly motivated to work with both children and young adults. School library media programs serve as the hub of educational activity in a school, addressing the information needs of the entire school curriculum. Excitement, creativity, and challenge characterize this particular field of librarianship.

The role of the school library media specialist is to manage a library media center at the elementary, middle, or high school level. Librarians in these positions are expected to wear many hats, including those of manager, teacher, collaborator, literacy advocate, technology specialist, and public relations expert.[1] Responsibilities are numerous, particularly due to the fact that most school libraries consist of only one or two full-time staff members. The library media specialist must act as the budget director, staff supervisor, purchaser, cataloger, archivist, and repairer of equipment. He or she is also responsible for teaching library skills and research skills to the student body as well as to the teaching faculty. He or she collaborates with the school's faculty to plan programs in support of the teaching curriculum and helps the school to achieve the learning standards required by each state. Since they are often the first ones called to solve computer or software problems, school media specialists must be up-to-date with the latest technology and must maintain database knowledge skills, Internet skills, and word processing skills, and must be able to teach those same skills to others.

The school library media profession has been growing steadily as parents and school administrators recognize the value of a well-funded, well-staffed school library media center. Studies have shown a direct correlation between the availability of quality library resources and student achievement. Students at schools with well-funded library media centers and with media specialists who play an instructional role in the curriculum tend to achieve higher average reading scores.[2] In addition, studies show that test scores rise in elementary and middle schools when library media specialists and teachers collaborate to promote information literacy. Scores also increase with the amount of time library media specialists spend training other teachers in the use of information technology.[3] All of these facts, gathered from various studies, are helping school library media specialists successfully lobby for additional funding for library resources. In the past, budgets for school libraries have generally been less than adequate. This unfortunate fact is rapidly changing. School administrators and communities are beginning to recognize that a strong library is an important investment in a child's education and that the school library media specialist is a necessary part of a school's learning environment.

CHILDREN'S SERVICES/YOUNG ADULT SERVICES LIBRARIANSHIP

Those who choose to specialize in children's librarianship in a public library setting are, in essence, assuming the responsibility for introducing, emphasizing, and endorsing literacy to children. Since public libraries in general are not geared solely toward children, it is the task of the public children's librarian to advocate for children and young adults in their libraries through a variety of services and to recognize and protect their rights as patrons.[4] These are heavy, demanding responsibilities, but they are part of what makes this field of librarianship so fulfilling.

Children's librarians and young adult librarians provide reference and research services to children and youth of all ages. They often serve parents and teachers as well. They act as readers' advisors by recommending books for different reading levels and interests. They may be involved in book and journal selection, departmental management, supervision of other staff members, budget management, committee work, maintenance of websites, and the preparation of bibliographies, pathfinders, and displays. Not only do these duties require extensive knowledge of current trends in children's literature, they also demand familiarity with child development and learning skills.

Librarians in these positions devote a large percentage of time to the planning and coordination of programs for children and young adults. Examples of such programs include story hours, summer reading programs, after-school library activities, writing workshops, family evenings, in-service workshops for teachers, lectures, tours, and outreach and public relations programs designed to promote children's library services throughout the community. Periodic evaluation of these programs and the implementation of the necessary changes to make them more effective is another important aspect of the job.

No matter the project, children's and young adult services librarians must be always conscious of their obligation to protect the rights of children as library patrons, to recognize and encourage diversity and, most important, to advocate for literacy.[5] Public libraries are in a unique position to expose children to large quantities of print and other meaningful resources. Studies have shown that activities such as summer reading programs not only encourage children to spend significant amounts of time with books, they also improve reading skills considerably. These kinds of programs also encourage parents to play greater roles in their children's literacy development.[6]

Children's and young adult librarians have an obligation to serve children well and to provide the best access to information possible. This doesn't mean that they can't have fun in the process. In fact, this may be the only field of librarianship that encourages silliness and laughter. In the midst of carrying out some heavy-duty responsibilities, it's okay to paint faces, play with macaroni, handle puppets, and sing silly songs once in a while.

SPOTLIGHTS

TONI BUZZEO
Library Media Specialist
Longfellow Elementary School
Portland, Me.

Toni Buzzeo

"Library media specialists are the beacons of literacy in a school. We are the people who live the belief that every child can be joyfully literate, and we work every day to ensure that this is so." Toni Buzzeo's compelling words vividly express the love she has for her job. As library media specialist at Longfellow Elementary School in Portland, Maine, Buzzeo is not only an advocate for literacy; she is also a sponsor and friend to teachers and students, and a benefactor for parents.

Buzzeo's job consists of four distinct roles. "First and foremost, I am both a teacher and instructional partner," she says. "I am also the information specialist for teachers, staff, parents, and students. Finally, I am the library's program administrator."

As teacher and instructional partner, Buzzeo focuses on student learning and achievement through collaboration with other teachers. "I believe that student success is best ensured by planning and teaching collaboratively with my classroom teaching colleagues, and I have always built library programs in my schools based on this belief." She is responsible for designing and planning new teaching units, reviewing and refining existing units, scheduling instructional use of the library, and team-teaching the instructional units.

In her role as information specialist, Buzzeo makes herself available to the members of the school community to answer informational needs. Her primary patrons are students in grades K–5. She considers teachers and staff to be equally important client groups. Parents of students, who are routinely encouraged to take books home, comprise another patron set.

As the library's program administrator, Buzzeo is responsible for "a constantly evolving program that includes instruction, literacy incentives, author/illustrator connections, and celebrations of the written word." She is in charge of all materials acquisitions, original cataloging, and massaging of existing cataloging. She plans library programs and events such as poetry festivals and the Maine Student Book Award program. In addition, she serves as co-chair of the library committee and assists her library education technician with her job and responsibilities as necessary. In her flexibly scheduled library, there is no strict daily routine. "The key is to meet all teaching obligations, then to respond to individual patron needs as they arise, and finally to fit in the program management tasks as time allows."

"Librarianship in an elementary school is a joy," says Buzzeo. "Because kids in early grades are so exuberant, some of the best moments in my days are spontaneous songs or recitations. I try to take a stint at the circulation desk every single day so that I have some time to just talk to kids in a relaxed way and to learn more about them and their interests and concerns." She loves to answer the question, "Can you recommend a book to me?" and is happiest when she hears students encouraging each other to read the books that they have enjoyed. For this reason, she is a strong advocate for the Maine Student Book Award program. "It give kids a common body of literature around which to communicate," she explains. "It's quite often that I hear kids gathered in certain areas of the library discussing the relative merits of the books in each collection. I often hop in and participate myself!"

One of Buzzeo's most touching experiences involved a kindergartener who would come to the library for information on sign language. Since the girl had a deaf mother, she would check out sign language books and print sign language information from the library's *World Book Encyclopedia* on CD-ROM. "Each time she came to the library, I encouraged her growth as an independent library user and handed her a book or two I thought she might enjoy, even though she claimed to have no interest in reading," recounts Buzzeo. "But she would always return the books unread." This went on for years, and by the time the child was in the fifth grade, Buzzeo was concerned but did not change her tactics. One memorable day, the girl came into the library with one of the recommended books, *Ella Enchanted* by Gail Carson Levine, and rather than dropping it into the return bin, she marched over to Buzzeo and said, "I loved this book!" She had read it and wanted to renew it so she could read it again. From that day forward, the child was a committed reader, visiting the library frequently, often daily, and discussing the books she read. Later that fall, Buzzeo asked her, "What happened? How did you become a reader after all this time?" "Mrs. Buzzeo," the girl replied, "I became a reader because you just kept putting a book into my hand all these years."

With stories like these under her belt, it's no wonder that, in 1999, Buzzeo was named the Maine Library Media Specialist of the Year. "That was one of the greatest honors of my life," she says.

Buzzeo has a B.A. in English and an M.A. in English language and literature from the University of Michigan. She worked as a teacher in community colleges in Michigan as well as in the External Degree Program at St. Joseph's College in Maine. "I also taught high school English for a few years before returning to my first love—library work," she says. She fell in love with libraries as a child and with library work while employed as a library page at the age of sixteen in her hometown of Dearborn, Michigan. "After working for a year as a children's librarian in Gorham, Maine, without the benefit of an M.L.I.S., I commenced my library degree studies at the University of Rhode Island while working as a library educational technician at an elementary school. I have since worked in several elementary schools in two more districts in Maine." She has been in her position at Longfellow Elementary School for the past ten years.

"The most exciting feature of my job," says Buzzeo, "is the opportunity to influence the thinking, the learning, and the reading enjoyment of students. I love the integral and important role I play in my students' lives. It is very important to me that students who have left my school continue to come back and see me, continue to build on their experiences in accessing information with me, continue to read and tell me what they are reading. It is a testament to my influence in their lives."

Like many librarians today, Buzzeo finds limited funding to be the most challenging part of her job. Her position is funded at three days a week, despite the fact that Maine State Library Guidelines recommend that elementary schools have a library media specialist available five days a week. "I'm always struggling with a shortage of time to accomplish the things I must accomplish in my four roles," she says.

Due to her passion for connecting children to authors and illustrators, Buzzeo makes an effort to host two or more author or illustrator visits to the school each year. "They are the highlight of our instructional calendar and are highly popular schoolwide," she says. Buzzeo herself is an author of children's books as well as professional books on teaching and librarianship. Her books for young readers include *Dawdle Duckling* and *The Sea Chest*. Being committed to sharing her passions and skills with the information community, she has written four professional books: *Collaborating to Meet Standards: Teacher/Librarian Partnerships for K–6*, *Collaborating to Meet Standards: Teacher/Librarian Partnerships for 7–12*, *35 Best Books for Teaching U.S. Regions*, and *Terrific Connections with Authors, Illustrators, and Storytellers*. In addition to speaking at schools around the country, she has been invited to be one of her own school's guest authors this year and looks forward to this event with great anticipation.

To keep up with changing technology, Buzzeo collaborates and shares information with other K–12 librarians in her district. She is a member of a number of professional organizations, including Beta Phi Mu: International Library Science Honor Society, American Library Association, American Association of School Librarians, Maine Educational Media Association, Maine Education Association, and National Education Association. She attends workshops and conferences and is frequently an invited speaker at the state, regional, and national level.

Buzzeo attributes her success as a librarian to a number of factors. "I am a person who is intensely interested in children. Because children sense this, they trust me, and they enjoy my company," she explains. "I am a skilled teacher who makes learning enjoyable and who sets a high standard that students rise to meet. I am, by nature, collaborative, a key element of successful school librarianship. Finally, I am passionate about children's literature as a reader, as a reviewer, and as a writer."

For those interested in a career as a library media specialist in an elementary school, Buzzeo says, "Have courage! Be prepared to struggle against outmoded program structures that include rigid scheduling, library-as-teacher-planning time, and resistance to change. Make a commitment to the goals of our national organization, AASL (American Association of School Librarians), to achieve a collaborative working relationship with teaching colleagues in an open, flexibly scheduled library media center that is rich in excitement and fun." She says that, unfortunately, elementary librarians are not in high demand since districts often focus their library staffing efforts at the high school level. Hence, elementary school library media specialist positions are highly prized and sought after.

"In many ways, being a librarian in this new millennium means what it always has: that one is the keeper of the storehouse of human knowledge, both in print and virtual," says Buzzeo. "It means that one protects the intellectual freedom of one's patrons and encourages their growth as information literate citizens. But it also means that one must tackle the bigger questions that technology has raised: Who owns the expression of ideas? Who has access to those ideas? How is that access provided and equalized in an economically unequal society?"

"Librarianship is, perhaps, the best job in the world," concludes Buzzeo. She may be biased, but there are many who will agree.

For more information about Toni Buzzeo's work as a library media specialist and as an author, visit her website at http://www.tonibuzzeo.com.

AMY DANIELS
Head Media and A/V Specialist
Airport High School
West Columbia, S.C.

"I feel that I am part teacher, part librarian, part technology guru, part computer technician, and part magician." In her position as media specialist for Airport High School in Columbia, South Carolina, Amy Daniels is a "jack-of-all-trades." She is responsible for maintaining a collection of print and nonprint materials to support and enhance the high school's teaching curriculum. She orders, catalogs, processes, and weeds books, collaborates with teachers to determine their book and audiovisual needs, manages the library's budget, offers workshops for teachers, provides reference and research aid, takes pictures and videos of school events, maintains the school's web page, and handles computer and software issues. At the end of her ten-hour workdays, if she's not changing overhead light bulbs or engaging in some other menial but necessary task, she sometimes finds a moment or two to actually read some of the books she has in her collection!

Daniels, whose staff consists of another media specialist and a secretary, finds herself struggling with numerous demands and a limited budget. "Our collection is very outdated, and our budget is shrinking," she says. In addition to books and audiovisual materials, Daniels must use her dwindling budget to pay for copier paper, overhead bulbs, supplies, toner for the printers, and all audiovisual repairs. "This year we decided to begin targeting one curriculum area to devote the majority of our budget to. Instead of trying to put out lots of small fires and never accomplishing that, we decided to put out one major fire each year. Our teachers seemed to like this idea. The first group was excited to be able to sit down with us and go through catalogs to pick out books." Next year, she and her staff plan to target a different curriculum area.

Daniels reads book and video reviews in order to match materials with the curriculum and the needs of the students. "We've really been pushing 'fun' reading," she says. "Most high school students are being required to read books that are chosen to support the curriculum, and they have often forgotten what it's like to just read for fun." She explains that, at the elementary school level, there are many reading programs developed to encourage fun reading. Unfortunately, these types of programs are not often utilized in the high school environment. Through encouragement, and by offering prizes, Daniels has been able to generate interest in this type of leisure reading. "More and more students are coming in just to find a good book."

Since she cannot predict what each workday will bring, Daniels doesn't have a specific day-to-day routine. "A school media specialist must be very flexible," she says. "Most days I go to work with a list of things I need to do, but by the end of the day I realize I have accomplished very little that was on my list. Teachers, students, and administrators drop by my office for many things, and each feels that his or her question is the most important. Therefore, I must often stop whatever I'm doing to help someone else. Most of the time I find this very rewarding, but there are days when I feel so far behind in my own work that I wonder why I'm doing this!"

Much of Daniels's time is spent troubleshooting computers and helping with software problems throughout the school. "Most media specialists are thought to be the ones to go to for technology and training updates," says Daniels. "We are often the first ones called whenever the computer acts funny. Most schools don't have full-time on-site computer technicians, so the media specialist is the one who gets all the pleas for help. We are often running around the campus checking computers and helping with software issues." The fact that she receives little to no direct training for these computer-related tasks doesn't stop her. "We usually learn quickly and through hands-on [experience]," she says. She and her staff offer mini-workshops for teachers whenever a new database or software package has been acquired. Daniels also teaches a class for students called Media Communication, in which students are responsible for recording and editing all the school's daily video announcements.

Daniels finds working with high school students extremely rewarding. "High school students are great," she says. "They are old enough to have acquired many skills, yet they are still young enough to be excited about learning. They are usually not the hardened group of kids portrayed in the media. The majority are really great kids who love to learn. The students I've been around like to feel that you really care for them; they are very helpful and like to be asked to help. Like elementary students, they need love and hugs and leadership." Daniels enjoys interacting with the students and particularly enjoys recommending books to them. "I love when students come by to tell me that they really liked that book I suggested, and could I recommend more? I like seeing our statistics each month. We are checking out more books, and more students are coming to the media center on their own. We must be doing something right when students use their free time to read, research, and learn."

The students, who range from those who are developmentally delayed to those who are taking college-level classes for credit, are generally well behaved. Daniels has specific rules regarding behavior in the library, and she sticks by them. Occasionally, though, students try to bend the rules. "The biggest problem we've encountered is 'love in the library,'" she says. "High school students are smart! Several times we've had students from different classes conspire to come to the media center at the same time—and it's amazing how they can find the one place we can't monitor! We've installed security cameras to help us monitor those hidden areas, and we've hooked up a VCR to record what happens. We try to be as visible as possible, and we ask lots of questions."

Daniels has strong feelings about the role of the high school's media center. "High school is often the last chance we have to reach students before they leave the educational setting," she says. "We try hard to make sure they have the skills needed, whether they are going to continue their education, enter the military, or enter the world of work. We try hard to make sure they have basic computer skills, basic research skills, and understand the importance of reading. We want to make sure they are able to locate the information they need. It's not necessary for them to know everything—they just need to know where to find the answers to whatever questions they may be asked." Unfortunately, Daniels finds that administrators don't often seem to realize the impact a media center has on the entire school. "Many principals (who, incidentally, control the budgets) don't have a clue about what really goes on in the media center." Daniels is often frustrated by the lack of support, and by the fact that things can quickly go from bad to worse when leadership of the school changes. She hopes someday for a boss who "realizes what wonderful things a library can offer."

With a B.A. degree in elementary education and a minor in special education/learning disabilities, Daniels began her career as a teacher of a learning disabled resource class in a middle school. After two years, she decided to go to library school. "I had worked in the library as a student aide during high school. Having been around books all my life, going to library school seemed to be the next course for me," she explains. It only took her one year to earn her M.L.S. from the School of Library and

Information Science at the University of South Carolina. Her first professional librarianship job was as a school media specialist in Newberry County, where she was responsible for the libraries of two schools. Since she had no help and horribly outdated collections, the experience was not a good one for her. "During library school we had heard horror stories of collections that had books telling about forty-eight states or that one day man would walk on the moon," she says. "Well, I *had* those books—and more! I even had two biographies on Martin Luther King Jr. and three on John F. Kennedy, and not one of them mentioned their assassinations!" Daniels pulled those books from the shelves and attempted to weed others, and in doing so received negative reactions from many teachers. "Being fresh out of library school and having so many ideas, I felt I was doing the right things for the students. But having so much negativity from the teachers was hard." Daniels lasted two years on the job and decided she couldn't go back.

Temporarily discouraged with the school system, she looked to public libraries and found a job with the Richland County Public Library (RCPL) system in Columbia. "I believe that the cross-training in public and school libraries was a very wonderful experience for me," she says. "I worked for ten years at RCPL, beginning as a children's librarian and then moving on to reference. I was also assistant branch manager, and those skills have been very helpful to me." When she needed a change after her public library experiences, Daniels once again considered working in a media center. This time she was hired into her current job at Airport High School and has been there ever since.

"I think that the different jobs I've had in public and school libraries have made me a more well-rounded media specialist," says Daniels. "I think that all too often people will go into the field of school media and stay for thirty years or more. I think they tend to stagnate and become too comfortable."

One of Daniels's biggest challenges is keeping up with changing technology. "Continuing education is vital," she says. "We must have courses offered to us that will give us a vision for our future. Right now, technology training is so very important." Since she is offered few training opportunities by her administration, Daniels reads as many professional journals as she can. She browses "tech" sites on the Internet, networks with other media specialists, and constantly asks questions. "I'd like to think I'm not being nosey—just inquisitive!" She also belongs to the South Carolina Association of School Librarians.

For those interested in careers as high school media specialists, Daniels says, "My best advice would be to keep your sense of humor. Always remember to laugh at yourself. Remember that Rome was not built in one day—you will not change/fix/update all that needs to be done by yourself. Learn how to delegate work. Don't try to stay late every day; remember that you need time away from school." As the mother of a ten-year-old daughter, she knows the value of time away from work. "Also, learn to say 'no.' It's easy to get caught in the trap of trying to please everyone and do everything just because you're asked. It's fine to let your administration know you can't help with some things." Daniels also stresses the importance of documenting everything.

"Being a media specialist is hard work and long hours," she says bluntly. "The pay is not the best, but the rewards are great. I love feeling I've made a difference in even one student's life. I wish I could encourage more people to think about the school media program. Even though I feel like I'm never caught up, I love it and look forward to going to work most days."

"With all the advances in technology, this is a wonderful time to be a media specialist in a high school," Daniels continues. "We have so many resources online and so many 'toys' to work with. It's great to have so much information at our fingertips. Students today have so many challenges, and we must give them the basis for them to build upon. If we teach them how to research, how to verify the information they find, and then how to put that information to use, then we've done our job. In my library we are known as CIC (Chicks in Charge), and we are a vital part of the school. We teach, we help, we encourage. We are information specialists."

MARY D'ELISO
Children's Librarian
Monroe County Public Library
Bloomington, Ind.

There are many days when Mary D'Eliso thinks to herself, "I get to do this for a living? Amazing!" She finds great satisfaction in her job as a children's librarian at Monroe County Public Library. "My job lets me work with kids

Mary D'Eliso

and others, lets me make crafts with them, tell them stories, put a long-sought book into their grateful hands, or help them find just the information they were looking for," she says.

D'Eliso is one of six children's librarians in the library's main branch. Her job as a member of the Children's Department is to help promote and provide services, materials, and information. "We provide information and guidance to patrons in the library, over the phone, through e-mail and fax—questions are coming from all directions!" she says. Her primary clientele are not necessarily children, as one might automatically assume. In fact, the patrons served by her department vary drastically in age and education level. "Though our target age is birth through sixth grade, the patrons who approach our desk are all ages," explains D'Eliso. "Parents are looking for read-aloud book recommendations or parenting issues; grandparents are looking for fun materials to share with their little ones; education majors are building text sets; teachers are working on units. Often adults use the children's department when they want to learn about a topic but don't want a complicated or academic treatment: how to knit, for instance, or the basic tenets of Islam. And, of course, kids approach the desk asking for books, software, videos, etc., either for information or pleasure."

D'Eliso finds that a challenging part of her job is being able to react to the wide range of queries from patrons whose education levels vary from none to doctoral level and beyond. "From the preschooler who wants a book that's 'scary-but-not-too-scary' to the patron who would like information about the cultural impact of the Cinderella tale and its variants, the librarian must be able to adapt to each patron's unique needs," she says.

D'Eliso tries to anticipate her patrons' needs by making information available before patrons even think to ask for it. She accomplishes this by preparing bibliographies, pathfinders, displays, and websites, thereby greatly improving the department's quality of service. She and her co-workers are also deeply involved with instruction, which is considered a component of reference services. "We're still at a time when many patrons do not know how to navigate online tools, and many of our clients struggle with the online catalog (think first-graders)," she explains. "We try to show them not only the information, but also how to get it." In addition, she is responsible for helping to develop the library's print and nonprint collections.

"Programming in its many forms is also an essential and fun part of the job," says D'Eliso. Members of her department are often called on to perform a wide variety of services both within the library and elsewhere. She is involved with preschool programs, school-age events, family evenings, in-services to teachers and daycare providers, PTO lectures, tours for preschoolers, research tours for older children, and large auditorium events. She frequently serves on committees, where she advocates for and raises public awareness of children's services, and she helps evaluate the effectiveness of the department's projects and programs. In her work, she refers often to departmental goals and to the library's mission statement to help facilitate decision making. "Referring back to our guiding documents helps us to gain scope, to prioritize, and to use our resources to their best advantage," she explains. "We must be versed in library policy when confronted with a concern, and we must be aware of how to react in emergency situations."

Since D'Eliso is service-oriented, it is in her nature to say "yes" to every request and to want to provide every conceivable service to every individual or group. "This is the most exciting part of my job, but it is also the one that challenges me the most," she says. "I can say from experience that when I have said 'yes' to too many requests, I'm usually less effective at the bulk of the tasks." This is when, by using them as filter for new ideas, the library's mission statement and departmental goals become most useful. "When we consider a new service or program, we try to ask ourselves, 'How does this further our mission?' Sometimes we follow up with, 'What are we going to give up to achieve this?'"

"I think that one way in which children's librarians often differ from other positions in public libraries is by the sheer breadth of the work," says D'Eliso. "We provide reference assistance, build and manage the collection, plan and execute programs, provide outreach services, serve on committees, consult with teachers and local agencies, construct web pages, assist in computer use, promote the library and reading. The list goes on. There is absolutely no time to sit at the reference desk and read, as we are often thought to do by those who don't use libraries!"

As a child, D'Eliso loved visiting public libraries. "I loved the wood, the smells, and especially all those books that contained so many thoughts," she says. At sixteen, she got her first job as a page in the County of Los Angeles Public Library (CoLAPL) system, where she found a mentor in the children's librarian, Renee Vasos Tobin. Throughout college, she worked as a desk clerk, then after graduating became a library assistant in the CoLAPL system. "This was a paraprofessional position but held with it a great responsibility in a small branch," she says. While there, she gained experience in reference work, children's programming, supervision, purchasing, budgeting, and management. After a while, she was ready to "take the big step" and decided to pursue her library science degree from Indiana University in Bloomington, where she was able to take classes in children's literature, young adult literature, children's programming, and storytelling. Ten months after graduating, she learned of an opening in the children's department of the main branch of the Monroe County Public Library. She got the job and has been there ever since.

In her years of service, D'Eliso has learned that the ability to adapt and to work in a strategic manner is central to the job of a children's librarian. "Other skills that make a good children's librarian," she says, "include communication skills in many forms, reference skills, a desire to be around people and to serve children, good knowledge of children's literature, the ability to multitask, creativity, the ability to manage a budget, storytelling skills, a desire to advocate for children, time management skills, decision-making skills, and everything else!" To keep up-to-date with these skills, she takes continuing education courses at conferences and attends training sessions for new tasks and systems. She takes courses at the School of Library and Information Science (where, incidentally, she occasionally teaches children's literature) and the Education School at Indiana University.

D'Eliso finds keeping up with technology to be a balancing act. "When I started working libraries, the next big thing in technology was a book catalog on microfiche," she recalls. "Can you imagine? The patron wants *Anne of Green Gables* and has to run the microfilm back to its beginning. The next book on a patron's list would inevitably be *Z for Zachariah* and they would patiently have to set the film whirring to the end of the reel! Today, libraries must respond to patron needs but also look to technology development in order to plan wisely for the future. In my role as children's librarian, I'm usually in a position to respond to technology rather than to initiate it. Which is a good thing, as I'm not exactly a techno-whiz!"

To D'Eliso, being a librarian in this new millennium means "staying on your toes." "The Internet has revolutionized our work," she says. "The finite set of tools we once had now seems infinite." She says that a librarian's sense of community has grown boundlessly, partially due to electronic discussion groups through which ideas and issues may be discussed, advice might be given, and reference help may be shared. "I feel connected to my colleagues around the world in ways I never had before. My circle of peers expands continually."

For those considering a career as a children's librarian in a public library, D'Eliso says, "Don't go into this job only because you love to read! A knowledge of, and appreciation for, literature is extremely useful. However, a love of books is not going to help you when someone is having trouble with the public printer, or when you serve on issues committees, or when you're dealing with a challenging patron." She stresses that a deep commitment to public service and a support of the unique role a public library plays in its community will contribute to long-lasting job satisfaction. "If one believes in a library that truly has something to offer everyone, that all are welcome, and that the library is 'the people's university,' he or she will be more likely to have a long-lasting, rewarding career. I'd encourage librarians to consider their role in their communities: what steps do they take to help keep citizens informed and engaged, to break down the many boundaries to library service which exist, to be a truly vital component to the lives of those in their communities?" In addition, D'Eliso believes in crafting one's own philosophy of service and personal mission statement in order to keep focused and to avoid burnout.

The job market for children's librarians in public libraries is strong, particularly for those who are willing to relocate. When job searching, D'Eliso's advice is to do what a librarian does best: research! "Look at a potential library system's web page to get an idea of their level of technology," she says. "See how much of the site is devoted to children's services. Observe their program schedule: is the library attempting innovative programming or just the basic story times? Do you get a sense that this library is an exciting, interactive place? Are the library's mission statement or children's department goals available?" In addition, she recommends checking newspaper indexes for references to articles about the public library system.

"For those who do land a job in children's services, I'd suggest that they find a mentor," says D'Eliso. "They may be lucky enough to find someone in their library. If not, maybe in the library system, or perhaps they could use the wisdom of a librarians' electronic discussion group to act in a mentoring role. The mentors I've had have provided me with inspiration, encouragement, and friendship."

"The field of children's librarianship has the potential to be immensely rewarding," D'Eliso concludes. "Traditional yet ever changing, the career is what you choose to make it. You may have to advocate, to educate your board and administration, but if you are committed to the career's tenets, you can go far."

Sally Leahey

SALLY LEAHEY
Reference/Young Adult Services Librarian
McArthur Library
Biddeford, Me.

With the title "reference/young adult services librarian," Sally Leahey sometimes thinks she was hired to develop a split personality. At McArthur Library in Biddeford, Maine, she divides her time between reference services and young adult services. Even though she often feels as though there are not enough hours in the day to fulfill all of her responsibilities in both areas, she knows that she is lucky to have the job that she does. She has one of only four public library positions specified as "young adult" in the entire state of Maine. At heart, the portion of her job that allows for frequent interactions with teenagers is her true calling.

Leahey came to the world of librarianship with a background in social work. After earning a B.A. in English, she went on to earn an M.S.W. from Boston University, with a concentration in child welfare. She worked for a number of years as a caseworker and an administrator of childcare programs in rural Maine, focusing her efforts on advocacy for children. She then moved on to early childhood work and university teaching, while also volunteering in both a public and an elementary school library. When an educational technician job in a small elementary school library was advertised, she applied and was hired.

"I remained at that first library job for nine years, and looked forward to going to work every day," says Leahey. "Although the pay was terrible, I was a one-person operation and was able to accomplish a great deal with the cooperation and respect of the entire school. Going into a facility where the dusty, musty books were arranged by size and chosen from donations, it was easy to very quickly make a dramatic difference. Faculty and staff were eager for any support and welcomed programming ideas wholeheartedly. Students viewed the library as both a resource and a refuge for academic and recreational use." The experience was a positive one. When Leahey and her family moved to Portland, Maine, she found a job as a library assistant at a suburban high school. While there, she enrolled in the University of Rhode Island Graduate School of Library and Information Studies and earned her degree in library science. Though she enjoyed the constant contact with high school students and the well-funded technology and print resources at the high school, she soon grew disheartened by the "tyranny of hall passes, study halls, and enforcement of school rules." She was then hired into her present job at McArthur Library.

"The seed of librarianship was probably planted when I was in elementary school and an avid library user," says Leahey. "A reading addict even at that age, my parents limited me to borrowing six books at a time each week, and one of those was *Sally Runs the Bookmobile*." She feels that her inclination to work in the social services arena can be partly attributed to reading fiction, which allowed her to experience emotions and interpersonal dynamics from diverse points of view. "When I burned out on social services administration, I remembered how much I had enjoyed organizing my daycare center's library and volunteering at local libraries. The prospect of working in libraries every day seemed like an ideal joining of avocation with vocation. Plus, I figured that I could draw on my social work skills as needed and forget them when they got in the way."

Leahey feels that her social work background is helpful when dealing with teenagers at the public library. "Perhaps it makes me more tolerant of some adolescent behaviors than other people might be," she explains. "I've seen such a range of troubled kids and the families from which they come that I might not be as shocked or judgmental as I would be otherwise. I know that nearly everybody says that they 'really like kids,' but I've found that I particularly enjoy some of the 'bad-actors' that others don't care for, and I get a kick out of trying to win those kids over." Though she has encountered teenagers who are less than likeable, she has learned that a good trait to have in her position is the capacity to laugh and to find others to laugh with her. "A sense of irreverence and acceptance of questioning authority also comes in very handy at times for feeling a kindredship with teenagers," she adds.

As the designated reference librarian, Leahey spends a lot of time staffing the reference desk. In addition to handling reference questions, she provides computer assistance to patrons and offers readers' advisory services. When not scheduled at the reference desk, she spends her time planning programs, selecting and ordering materials, and attending meetings.

"Fairly routine programs might include my weekly 'Teen Space,' in-school booktalks, book discussion groups, and teen advisory group (TAG) meetings," she says. "My TAG has assisted in the planning of all special programs. Examples include teen concerts featuring teen rock bands, an after-hours LAN computer game night, a graphic novel workshop, a schoolwide survey, an ongoing poetry project, a rotating traveling book box for the local YMCA, and a bookstore shopping spree for the TAG. One of the more unusual projects was a pizzathon organized to raise money for the high school media center." Leahey is thankful that she has a lot of autonomy in providing young adult services and that she enjoys a generous budget that allows for healthy collection development.

"One of the most satisfying aspects of working in the public library setting is the diversity of the clientele," says Leahey. "While I must confess that my heart is with the teenagers, I enjoy contact with elderly and very young users as well. There is still a significant population in this community that has not yet learned to use computers or does not own a PC, so that public computer access remains a major role for the library. One of the more gratifying accomplishments in a day can be the successful introduction of computer use to a patron who has never before been able to do an Internet search or send an e-mail message." Leahey also enjoys the challenge of finding just the right book for a teenager who claims to hate reading, or discovering the right answer to an impossible reference question. "Probably the best challenge is to win over a patron of any age who isn't crazy about the library or even life in general." The most frustrating aspect of her job is the lack of tolerance for diversity that is sometimes found in a public library setting.

To network with colleagues and to keep up with new resources and programming ideas, Leahey attends professional conferences whenever possible. "I find that conferences energize me while giving practical day-to-day suggestions about both reference and young adult work," she says. "Two years ago I received an award from ALA's New Members Round Table and 3M to finance my attendance at the national ALA conference in San Francisco, which opened my eyes to just how much ALA has to offer." She is a member of ALA's Young Adult Library Services Association (YALSA) and serves on the Popular Paperbacks for Young Adults Committee.

"Maine has a very active and supportive library community that offers an annual conference, periodic professional development opportunities, regional library networks and consultation, a springtime Reading Round-up, and a busy [electronic discussion list]," says Leahey. "The New

England Library Association's annual conference is another welcome opportunity for training, and its spring symposium about children's and young adult literature is always stimulating and informative." Leahey is also active on a number of electronic discussion groups dealing with service to young adults, including YALSA-Bk, AdBooks, and Booktalking.

In library school, Leahey took courses pertaining to children's literature, public library services for children and young adults, and electronic resources for children and young adults. However, she feels that exposure to the young adult population is just as important as formal training. To those interested in jobs as young adult services librarians in public libraries, she advises hanging around teenagers as much as possible and volunteering in a library setting serving that age group. "To tell the truth, I think attitude is at least as important as specific skills," she adds. "Willingness to try new approaches to find just the right resources, persistence to stick with patron requests, expressed genuine interest in patron needs, curiosity, flexibility, and overall good humor are crucial in most library interactions. These qualities can't be taught in library school and to me are much more important than any degree. I sure can't claim to always model these behaviors, but when things go well in my work it's because of the quality of personal interaction at least as much as because of any learned skill. I think that a master's degree is only one part of being a successful librarian."

Regarding the challenges all librarians face in this age of technology, Leahey says, "I definitely think that we're all going to need to move along at least with the times, if not ahead of them. We need to be resource enablers, connecting people with the information and recreational literature they request, regardless of the format. I expect that politics and technology will cause heightened challenges to privacy and freedom of access in the coming years. Librarians will need ongoing vigilance to safeguard our patrons' rights and freedoms."

SAMPLE JOB DESCRIPTIONS

School Library Media Specialists (K–12)

Environment

School library media specialists manage libraries in elementary, middle, or high school libraries. They are given a variety of responsibilities, from the ordering of books to the management of a yearly budget, and they must work closely with the teaching faculty to ensure that library services and materials support the school's curriculum. Their patrons include school children, teaching staff, teaching aides, administrative staff, school board members, other librarians, parents, and the community. School library media specialists generally work alone or with one or two assistants, depending on the library's size and budget.

Responsibilities

Supervise all library personnel

Manage the library's budget

Order, catalog, and process print and nonprint materials

Teach library and research skills to students and teachers

Collaborate with teaching faculty to plan library programs and order materials in support of the teaching curriculum

Encourage literacy and act as readers' advisor to students

Prepare bibliographies, pathfinders, and displays

Maintain the library's website

Maintain the library's computers and audiovisual equipment

Troubleshoot computer and software problems schoolwide

Keep abreast of new technologies, and assume a leadership role in the provision and application of various technologies facilitating teaching and student learning skills

Maintain database searching skills and general database knowledge, Internet skills, and word-processing skills

Advocate for library programs to encourage adequate funding

Participate in schoolwide committees

Evaluate library programs

Maintain detailed use statistics for library resources

Education and Training

A master's degree in library and information science from an ALA-accredited institution is required. Completion of a teaching certification or licensure program is required, but requirements differ slightly from state to state.

Recommended Memberships

American Library Association (ALA)

American Association of School Librarians (AASL), a division of ALA

State or regional associations for school librarians

Children's Services/Young Adult Services Librarians (Public Libraries)

Environment

In public libraries, children's services librarians and young adult services librarians are charged with providing reference, research, and readers' advisory services to children and young adults. Duties range from book and journal selection to the planning and coordination of programs and services. Other responsibilities are dependent upon the size of the department and the number of staff involved but often include management or administrative duties.

Responsibilities

Manage reference services for the department

Coordinate young readers' advisory services

Plan and execute programs and services geared toward children or young adults

Supervise departmental employees

Select books, journals, and other media for purchase

Manage departmental budget

Prepare bibliographies, pathfinders, and displays for the department

Participate in librarywide committees

Maintain departmental statistics

Keep abreast of new technologies and databases, especially as related to children or young adult library services

Teach library skills, research skills, and computer searching skills to patrons

Maintain the portion of the library's website dealing with children or young adult services

Advocate for children's literacy and for adequate departmental funding

Evaluate departmental programs

Education and Training

A master's degree in library and information science from an ALA-accredited institution is required. Additional training in children's or young adult literature or providing library services to children or young adults is recommended but not required.

Recommended Memberships

American Library Association

Young Adult Library Services Association (YALSA), a division of ALA

Association for Library Service to Children (ALSC), a division of ALA

Public Library Association (PLA), a division of ALA

Notes

1. Librarians in the Twenty-First Century: K–12 Librarians, 2000, available at http://www.istweb.syr.edu/21stcenlib/who/k-12.html. Accessed 3 February 2003.
2. Keith Curry Lance, "The Impact of School Library Media Centers on Academic Achievement," *School Library Media Quarterly* 22, no. 3 (spring 1994): 167–70, 172.
3. Keith Curry Lance, Marcia J. Rodney, and Christine Hamilton-Pennell, *How School Librarians Help Kids Achieve Standards* (Denver: Library Research Service, 2000).
4. Marisa H. Grijalva, A Code of Ethics for Children's Librarians in Public Libraries, 2002, available at http://www.u.arizona.edu/~mhg. Accessed 3 February 2003.
5. Ibid.
6. Donna Celano and Susan B. Neuman, *The Role of Public Libraries in Children's Literacy Development: An Evaluation Report* (Harrisburg: Pennsylvania Library Association, 2001).

CHAPTER 3

Academic Librarianship

Academic librarianship is by far the most eclectic area of librarianship. Work settings vary widely, from small community college libraries to major research libraries within universities. Academic libraries primarily serve the academic community of the institution, which includes undergraduate students, graduate students, faculty, administration, and staff. Smaller college libraries may focus on serving the student body by supporting the curriculum, while larger university libraries not only support the curriculum, but also furnish graduate students and faculty with material to support their research.[1] Some academic libraries might even serve the needs of the general public.

Opportunities vary according to the interests and expertise of individual librarians. While some academic librarians are involved with management or administration, others may work in reference, instruction, computer and information systems, circulation, acquisitions, cataloging, serials, government documents, archives, subject specialization, or collection management. Traditionally, it has been the norm for academic librarians to work exclusively in a particular field within either public or technical services. Today, many academic librarians divide their work among several areas of expertise. The cataloger, for example, may work at the reference desk for a certain number of hours per week, or the reference librarian may spend time selecting subject-specific titles for acquisition.

The academic environment, culturally and educationally rich, has its roots in scholarship and the life of the scholar. As such, the academic librarian is considered a scholar in his or her own right and must fulfill certain scholarly expectations. On many campuses, academic librarians are appointed faculty and are able to secure tenure. As faculty members, they are expected to pursue further formal education, to do research, and to publish. These activities are expected to be accomplished on top of the librarian's normal workload and are therefore sometimes considered burdensome. Most academic librarians, however, welcome the challenge and are rightfully proud of their positions as productive faculty within the academic community.

Technology is another challenge that academic librarians must face on an almost daily basis. "Increased use of information technology has greatly influenced the evolution of academic libraries."[2] No longer is the academic librarian viewed as a collector of books but rather as a gateway to information. Academic librarians must stay abreast of new technologies in order to provide the most up-to-date information to students, faculty, and researchers. Not only must they be proficient in database searching, web technology, and systems maintenance and administration, they must also be able to teach these same skills to library patrons and co-workers.

In short, "the academic librarian is a jack-of-all-trades, knowledgeable in the rudiments of research methods and reference tools; skilled in the art of negotiation between administrators, faculty, students, and community organizations; accepting of technological change; committed to the preservation and stewardship of historic collections; versed in the complications of copyright law; involved in the governance of the profession and always present to the students. Academic librarianship is a dynamic field, well-suited to innovation and ingenuity. The successful academic librarian is one who wears each of these hats with honor."[3]

SPOTLIGHTS

Anne C. Moore

ANNE C. MOORE
Head of Reference Services
W.E.B. Du Bois Library
University of Massachusetts

"The availability of a librarian to assist users anytime they need support is vital to the role of libraries today. As users visit our facilities less frequently and use our resources digitally, they expect and need assistance in interpreting these new collections on their schedule rather than ours." Anne C. Moore, head of Reference Services at W.E.B. Du Bois Library, takes on the challenge of providing reference services in the areas of social sciences and the humanities to the University of Massachusetts twenty-four hours a day, seven days a week. Naturally, nobody could carry out this feat single-handedly. She supervises a staff of eight full-time librarians, three full-time classified staff, six part-time librarians, and several student assistants. It is Moore's responsibility to ensure that one or more of these trained professionals are available to assist users at any time and through any means, whether it be by e-mail, by telephone, at the reference desk, or via virtual reference services.

In addition to managing reference services, Moore is also responsible for government documents and works closely with other library departments to improve service to users in general. "I serve on library committees, such as the Web Advisory Group, Electronic Resources Advisory Group, Digital Initiatives Task Force, Senior Management Group, and many ad hoc groups for specific projects," she says. Moore serves on the Graduate Council and Academic Priorities Council for the University, chairs the Academic Liaison Program for the library, and chairs the Research, Instruction, and Outreach Committee of the Five Colleges. Five Colleges is a consortium of the libraries of the University of Massachusetts Amherst, Amherst College, Hampshire College, Mount Holyoke College, and Smith College.

"As a night person, I prefer to stay later in the evening to catch up on all e-mails, complete projects, and prepare for the next day rather than come in early in the morning," says Moore. "Consequently, I arrive between 8:45 and 9:15 each morning, depending on the time of the first meeting of each day." After her scheduled meetings with committees or individuals, Moore deals with any emergency issues that have arisen.

"Many assignments come by e-mail late in the morning," she explains. "Throughout the day, I try to keep up with the incoming e-mail, responding to quick questions and adding those that require consultation or additional research to my to-do list." Often she plans to work on a major project only to be confronted with a reference crisis, whereupon the project is placed on temporary hold. "As a department head and chair of a variety of library committees, I have one to four meetings to plan per week," she adds.

"E-mail is simultaneously a facilitator of communication and an incredible time absorber," Moore states. "In a large organization, an environment in which hundreds of e-mails arrive each day augmented by electronic discussion threads and the seemingly unavoidable spam, it can be extremely difficult to keep up with the important e-mails. While e-mail absorbs several hours out of each workday, it makes it possible to get the word out quickly on many topics to just the right people."

As a supervisor, Moore maintains an open-door policy. "I try to walk by and chat briefly with each person every day," she explains. "My door is open most of the time and folks stop in to ask questions many times each day." She makes the most of having her workstation situated right next to the copy machine by chatting with people while they are making copies. "Within the library, I try to facilitate problem-solving by carrying information between parties to smooth the way for change," she says.

Moore is often involved with cooperative projects that she finds to be both stimulating and rewarding. One such project involved participating in a "chat reference pilot" involving all five University of Massachusetts campuses (Amherst, Boston, Dartmouth, Lowell, and Worcester.) Specialized software was used to provide chat reference service from 1 to 5 P.M. Monday through Friday. "Each campus covered one afternoon per week for the entire library system," she explains. "With the software, we could chat, push pages, and go into each other's databases while assisting patrons. It was an excellent opportunity to learn about each others' collections and services while mastering the protocols of chat reference."

Moore is currently involved in another pilot program with the Boston Library Consortium. The program, called "BLC Ask 24/7," provides 24/7 reference using sophisticated software that allows librarians to travel with the user through the Internet and follow them into databases they are eligible to access in order to provide support. "We send screenshots, Word documents, spreadsheets, or presentations that provide customized guidance," she says. "We are digitally with the user in his quest for information."

Moore has also worked diligently to help University of Massachusetts Libraries produce web-based, subject-specific research guides for each discipline. This is an in-depth, cooperative effort involving librarians, subject specialists, and student testing. Moore serves as web-content editor for this ongoing project, which thus far has resulted in the production of a number of research guides on Afro-American studies, anthropology, business, career resources, economics, education, law, music, September 11, 2001, sociology, and many others.

Moore came to the W.E.B Du Bois Library with a background made rich by a variety of work experiences. She was exposed to libraries at a young age through her mother, who was active as a public library trustee. "I accompanied my mother to numerous functions and developed a lifelong love of libraries," Moore says. "My early experience in public libraries focused on the people who ran, worked in, and cared about pub-lic libraries rather than just the materials that populated them. Although my mother was not a librarian, I learned to understand and appreciate librarians as people in all their variety with dedication to bringing reading material and information to people. Becoming a professional in libraries was a natural outgrowth for the daughter of a public library trustee."

Moore attended Duke University and earned a dual major in Spanish and English. After graduation, she took a job at Duke University's Perkins Library as a library clerk, where she filed cards in the subject card cata-log. Gradually, she acquired other duties such as copy cataloging, editing records in OCLC, and verifying records in the acquisitions system. "All these were duties that required focus and attention to detail, personal traits that I had in quantity. At this time, I enjoyed interacting with things rather than people because of shyness."

Moore soon moved to the position of library assistant senior for Subject Control, where she supervised filers and revisers for the subject card catalog, performed copy cataloging, and trained new employees in the use of OCLC. "Sitting just a few feet from where Anne Rice (author of *The Mummy* and numerous vampire books) had worked only a couple of years earlier as Russian cataloger made me feel like there were no lim-its to what all of us could achieve if we worked diligently and creatively," she says. "In this second classified position, I learned the satisfaction of maintaining accurate records, the power and versatility of the card cata-log, the warmth of people who work in libraries, and the challenges and rewards of supervision."

Once mastering the responsibilities of her job, Moore decided to enroll in library school at the University of North Carolina at Chapel Hill. "Library school was a joy," says Moore. She was granted a graduate assistantship in Latin American Bibliography in the Wilson Library and learned acquisitions searching of Spanish, Portuguese, and Italian materi-als. Later, she learned copy and original cataloging of media and serials as well as monographs. "I immersed myself in library school," she says. "My previous library experience provided a framework to support the knowl-edge presented in coursework and made it easier to understand and retain new principles. The simultaneous experience in the assistantship rein-forced course content and provided examples to contribute in classes."

As the spouse of an Air Force pilot, Moore and her family moved around quite a bit. After graduating from library school, she developed her skills by working a variety of jobs and by volunteering at public or school libraries in each new city. "This allowed me to meet other librarians, learn about the town, and help out the community," she explains. "Many times I continued the volunteer work after beginning full-time employment."

In Tucson, Arizona, Moore worked in the cataloging department of the University of Arizona. As the technical services' liaison to the reference department, she had the opportunity to train other library staff and to become involved in reference. "The joy of assisting patrons in finding information and teaching in the library instruction program ignited a desire to become a public service librarian," she says.

In Suffolk, England, Moore worked as an educational administrator at Embry-Riddle Aeronautical University while pursuing a master's degree in education in counseling. In Hawaii, she taught as a substitute teacher, and in Virginia she established an academic branch library for George Mason University Libraries. In Alamogordo, New Mexico, she began working on her doctorate in educational management and development at New Mexico State University (NMSU), at the same time working as electronic resources librarian at NMSU Library. Later, she became library director of the Alamogordo branch of NMSU. She completed her doctoral dissertation, selecting assessment of information literacy instruction as the focus of her research. Finally, she accepted her current position at the W.E.B. Du Bois Library at the University of Massachusetts.

"The most challenging aspect of my job is motivating staff to adapt to changes in technology, the organization, and resources," says Moore. "Academic libraries in particular attract people who are extremely precise and thorough in their work, but not necessarily eager to embrace change with gusto. This aspect of my job is also the most rewarding. Motivating people to assist others more efficiently and effectively is the key. Taming technological tools to improve services yields satisfied users who are eager to return."

Moore finds the most difficult aspect of her job to be dealing with the politics prevalent in a university setting. "Persuading nonbelievers that a particular course is the best (consensus-building) takes dedication and finesse. Deciding how to effectively present issues that might evoke a contentious response, to dispel the reaction, is a tricky proposition. You succeed on some occasions and fail miserably on others. Developing experience over time, having a supportive mentor, and attending management courses all help the budding manager develop these skills."

To keep up with changing technology, Moore subscribes to electronic discussion groups relevant to her areas of expertise, surfs the Web for vendor sites, and "hangs out at the booths" when attending conferences. She also reads professional literature and attends training sessions whenever possible to develop her skills with software and other applications. "In libraries as in most careers, it is essential to want to embrace new knowledge," she says. "If you don't keep pace with the new technology, collections, resources, services, and ideas of the profession, more innovative librarians will step up to take your place. Consequently, I attend as much training as I possibly can. When the organization adds a new software package, I attend all of the workshops that are offered as soon as possible. Then I force myself to use the software immediately and until I feel comfortable. Don't even wait a day!"

Moore is a member of the American Library Association and its Association of College and Research Libraries, and has joined regional library associations in each area she has resided. "As scholars in a particular field," she says, "librarians should belong to at least one discipline-specific organization to keep up with issues and changes within the subject area."

Moore says that the most important attributes of an academic reference librarian include love of learning, flexibility, dedication, organizational skills, attention to detail, precision, efficiency, empathy, caring, and tenacity. Skills involving research, technology, management, communication, and innovation contribute to success in the career. "The long-term prospects in the job market for reference librarians are bright," she says. "How we organize, access, and provide information will continue to change constantly for the foreseeable future, and people will need assistance in locating information. That's job security."

"Despite difficult economic times that squeeze money from public services like public and academic libraries, citizens and scholars value high-quality information that can sometimes only be located through library resources and with the assistance of library staff," says Moore. "The emergence of databases and dynamically created web pages increases our capability to organize, customize, and deliver information such as primary sources formerly hidden in archives and paper backfiles. Libraries can now make enormous quantities of powerful new information available and facilitate its use. It's an exciting time to be a librarian."

Mary Dabney Wilson

MARY DABNEY WILSON
Director of Cataloging
Texas A&M University Libraries

"A cataloger's role is fundamental to the success or failure of information systems." Having been involved with cataloging for the past thirty-five years, Mary Dabney Wilson speaks these words with the wisdom of experience and the conviction of a dedicated cataloger.

As the director of cataloging at Texas A&M University, Wilson is responsible for the management of the cataloging department and the supervision of nine professional librarians and twenty-five support staff. "At this point in my career, I do not catalog on a daily basis," she explains. "My position is largely managerial." Her daily responsibilities involve personnel management, revision and documentation of procedures, training of staff, consulting on unusual cataloging problems, supervision of workflow, and handling special cataloging projects as they arise. In addition, Wilson is the local coordinator of NACO (Name Authorities component of the Program for Cooperative Cataloging) and is involved with NACO training as well as the periodic review of submitted authority records.

"Other than managing cataloging operations, what a head of cataloging does is largely the function of the institutional directions in which the cataloging processes take place," says Wilson. "In this library, what may be unique is the role cataloging has in achieving our institutional goals related to service quality. As someone experienced in the systems of access, I am called upon to work with others in the library's management team to achieve our goal of services that support a much more self-sufficient library user. The national trend of lower reference and in-house circulation transactions along with the results of our service quality surveys have focused our efforts toward accuracy of records, both catalog and patron records, and creating services that are more intuitive."

An example of such a service in which Wilson is directly involved is the development of a completely redesigned web presence for the Texas A&M University Libraries. "We are using a content management system for this new effort," she explains. The one area in which she is most involved relates to developing an automated presentation of subject content for electronic resources using classification. "It's exciting to be able to contribute to my library's efforts in transforming our service goals and our website."

Wilson sees academic library catalogers as serving at least two primary clienteles: the library catalog user as well as other catalogers in the national and international cataloging community. "The product of a cataloger's expertise is an original cataloging record, integrated and related to other records in a catalog," she expounds. "The clientele served are the users of that record, which includes the students, faculty, and staff of the institution as well as anyone querying that catalog from anywhere in the world. Seen from another perspective, other catalogers are the potential users of the record because of the shared cataloging environment in which most academic libraries find themselves. I've often thought that catalogers are unappreciated schizophrenics, trying always to accommodate local needs while meeting international standards."

Having studied art and history as an undergraduate, Wilson did not at first anticipate a career in librarianship, much less cataloging. "I wish I could say that I knew from childhood that I wanted to be a cataloger, as that might indicate a degree of purpose or single-mindedness in pursuit of a profession," she says. "However, perhaps like many others, I more or less stumbled upon it." After graduating with her degree in art, Wilson worked as a cashier selling tickets to fine arts performances at the University of Texas at Austin. Soon afterward she took a position in the cataloging department of the university library and was thus initiated into the world of academic librarianship.

"Those were the days of cards, specifically depository cards sent by the thousands to certain academic libraries by the Library of Congress and filed into 'depository catalogs' of tremendous size," she says. "Before online utilities like OCLC or RLIN, these cards were used as cataloging copy." Wilson read those depository cards before filing them and was fascinated, finding that they "represented the full breadth of human interests and pursuits." In short, she was hooked, and her "temporary" position became the first building block in a fulfilling career.

After her paraprofessional cataloging position at University of Texas at Austin, Wilson worked in a similar position at UCLA. "After over ten years, I had advanced about as far as I could without the professional degree and so decided that obtaining it would be a logical next step." She enrolled in the library school at the University of Texas at Austin, where, in addition to the core courses, she took beginning and advanced cataloging as well as a course in classification systems. Since graduating with her master's in library science, her professional positions have included seven years as a lab instructor assisting in the teaching of cataloging courses at the University of Texas at Austin, three years as an authority control librarian at UCLA, and almost nine years as head of Bibliographic Control at the University of Texas at Arlington. "I have been director of cataloging at Texas A&M University for six years. My entire professional career has been associated with cataloging, and most of that has been in academic libraries."

Wilson finds great satisfaction in the various aspects of her job, from participating in the library's service goals to her involvement in ALCTS (ALA's Association for Library Collections and Technical Services) Cataloging and Classification Section. "Another gratifying feature is the recruitment of new catalogers. Since coming here I have recruited or been closely involved in the recruiting of four very talented catalogers new to the profession."

The most difficult aspect of Wilson's job is struggling with multiple demands on her time. "I seem to have the nearly constant concern that I have left something important undone," she says. "Also, writing and research don't come particularly easy to me and those endeavors are part of this package." Because Texas A&M University librarians have faculty status, they are expected to spend time engaging in research and writing for publication. "This isn't unique within academic libraries, but it was unique to me when I came here after over nineteen years in other professional positions where professional service was highly valued but publication was not required. Here, peer-reviewed publication is definitely required."

To keep up with cataloging technological changes, Wilson reads articles and participates in electronic discussion groups. She belongs to numerous professional associations and attends meetings and continuing education sessions regularly. She participates in the Program for Cooperative Cataloging (PCC), supports the Serials Cataloging Cooperative Training Program (SCCTP) of CONSER, and takes advantage of opportunities for training offered by ALCTS. "I believe that through my participation in these associations I have made and will continue to make contributions that will further cataloging cooperation," she says.

To those interested in careers as cataloging librarians, Wilson says, "The best advice would be to take as many courses that emphasize theory of information organization and access, especially courses in classification, subject analysis, and indexing." She says that the job market is good for catalogers with specialized experience such as in serials, electronic resources, maps, and archival and special formats cataloging. For those inexperienced librarians, Wilson encourages participation in internships or practicums while in library school. "My institution and others have a commitment to hiring and developing new catalogers and regularly post vacancies at the entry level, but some experience is always a plus."

Because of the frequency in which information content changes, Wilson feels that cataloging librarians today are faced with significant challenges. "I'm certain that librarians of every decade have asserted that theirs are times of great change," she says. "It is with some trepidation that I express the same for this time as well. The case I would make is that electronic information and technology have so transformed the information environment that it is hardly recognizable to someone who, like me, started off in the tranquil, slower times of depository card catalogs. At least in the print environment, you had a fixed object to describe and relate to other physical objects. Now, information content can and does change frequently. Grasping the mutability of the content, in order to organize it, to make it accessible, and to relate it to other information in a meaningful way is a tremendous, but attainable, stretch of the systems libraries and librarians have devised."

"While some problems of organization are new," Wilson continues, "many are the very same ones catalogers have been dealing with for a century: description, controlled vocabulary, multiple versions, subject analysis, data definition, record structure, metadata, etc. Many, if not most, of the skills developed over the last century in building great catalogs are just as applicable in this era of electronic information."

JOHN P. BLOSSER
Head, Serials Department and Coordinator of Acquisitions Services
Northwestern University Library

Armed with a degree in interior design, an enjoyment of business, and years of experience working in libraries, John Blosser molded a niche for himself in the world of librarianship. As head of the Serials department and coordinator

John P. Blosser

of Acquisitions Services at Northwestern University Library, Blosser has found work that keeps him busy and intellectually satisfied. He is responsible for the management of the Serials department and oversees all acquisitions activities. Included in his responsibilities is the complex task of handling the licensing and statistical tracking of all the library's electronic resources. "My role in the information community is to get information resources in the building for processing, or to get them 'plugged in' for use," he says. Blosser also works on budget management, coordinates the policies and upgrade issues for the acquisitions module of the library's management system, and serves on committees dealing with electronic resources, acquisitions, and finance. Thanks to his interest in design, he also finds himself involved with space planning, building renovations, and storage issues.

"The most exciting feature of my job is the business side of acquisitions," says Blosser. "I enjoy working with people and accomplishing tasks." He often deals directly with publishers and serials agents, and he enjoys the interaction.

"There are generally no two days alike," he says. At present, he is involved with building renovations and must deal with different priorities each day. "The daily Serials department work includes ordering and paying for electronic resources and making sure staff responsible for linking to these resources know they can do so. I help with linking as well. I also will order and pay for special purchases, usually purchases on special endowed funds, or higher priced items which selectors will want to be tracked. I manage a database of the electronic databases and journals we acquire, or in the case of the journals, those titles to which we have access because we subscribe to the print [version]." On any given day, Blosser may handle various database or journal access problems; he may be required to peruse intricate user licenses; he may need to answer acquisitions questions from selectors or staff members of the acquisitions unit; or he may attend a Technical Services meeting or one of various other meetings.

"The most difficult work is the maintenance of access to online resources," Blosser says. Electronic links can break for many reasons, and he knows he is not alone in the struggle to keep them active. Blosser also gets frustrated with e-mail. "The volume is very high," he explains, "and the venue has prompted people to expect an immediacy of response that is not always possible during a busy day."

Most of Blosser's work experience has involved libraries. He worked at a public library while pursuing his undergraduate degree in fine arts.

After graduation, he worked in his first academic library at Ohio State University, performing quick cataloging in the technical services department. Technical services work seemed to attract him, for he continued to work in that area as his career progressed. After moving to Chicago, he began working as a serials cataloger at Northwestern University Library. Shortly afterward, while back in school for an associate degree in interior design, Blosser took a part-time position in cataloging, handling series standing orders receipts. He continued to gain experience in various technical services positions, trying out such jobs as gift processing and bibliographic searching for ordering. He also worked in an association library as well as an art museum library. Finally realizing that professional library work was his calling, Blosser enrolled at the University of Illinois at Urbana-Champaign and earned his M.S.L.S.

After graduation, Blosser took temporary work at an association library until he learned of a half-time grant position at Northwestern University Library. He applied and became the cataloger of newspapers from Africa for the prestigious Melville J. Herskovits Library of African Studies at Northwestern. Another half-time position was added to expand his cataloging to other serials for the library. "A couple of years later, I began working closely with the head of the then-named Serials and Acquisitions Services on electronic processing. This work included ordering, paying for, tracking, and helping to negotiate licenses for databases and electronic journals," Blosser explains. "When the head position became vacant, I applied and was selected for the position."

Blosser is a member of the American Library Association (ALA) and the North American Serials Interest Group (NASIG). He regularly attends the NASIG annual conference and periodically attends ALA as well as the Charleston Conference: Issues in Book and Serial Acquisition. He also monitors a number of electronic discussion groups such as SERIALST, NASIG, ACQNET, and CIC-Acquisitions.

Blosser is a big advocate of acquisitions and serials work. "I would recommend that librarians interested in serials/acquisitions librarianship work in [as many] different areas of technical services as they may," he says. "Understanding cataloging will help with management issues of serials acquisitions and processing. Serials by their nature can bring problems and exceptions. One must not be easily frustrated by the need for handling exceptions. For acquisitions, someone with a mind for detail and who can be fiscally responsible will probably enjoy the work. A person who enjoys working with others may enjoy acquisitions work. Working with licensing is also a very good experience to have on a resume." Blosser also says that a firm understanding of technical services in general is important, as well as computer skills and Web experience.

Blosser feels that the technology involved with accessing information is a big challenge to all librarians today. "There is so much more information through which to search, the future seems almost overwhelming," he says. "The speed at which we all need to learn new things and adapt is increasing. Improvements to database interfaces require reorientation to what was once familiar. Coping with change is one of the biggest challenges I face because there is no longer time to get comfortable at a common ground before I need to move on up to the next level."

Blosser concludes, "To be a librarian in the new millennium means we will continue to help people access the information they need, but do so in our resolute, verifiable way in order to help assure the quality and relevance of the information to the patrons' needs."

John F. Dean

JOHN F. DEAN
Director, Department of Preservation and Collection Maintenance
Cornell University

Not many librarians can claim that they made their career choices at the age of eleven. John Dean, a native of Yorkshire, England, can do just that. At that early age, he earned a scholarship to the Municipal School of Arts and Crafts in Oldham, England (a branch of the Royal College of Art), where he took general art and bookbinding courses for four years. At the age of fifteen, he began a six-year bookbinding apprenticeship at the Oldham firm of Lee Whitehead Ltd., a company involved in conservation work. While there, he learned the technology of bookmaking, including how to produce complex bindings.

Following his apprenticeship, Dean served for two years in the military, then worked at the bindery of the Manchester Central Library, one of the largest municipal library systems in the world. Shortly after being hired, he was promoted to head of the bindery department and began teaching in the evenings at the University of Manchester Institute of Science and Technology and Her Majesty's Prison Strangeways. Ten years later, Dean's career brought him to Chicago, where he worked for five years at the bindery at Newberry Library. At the same time, he obtained his M.A. in library science from the University of Chicago.

"I then followed my former boss to the Johns Hopkins University, where I had drafted a plan for the future preservation and conservation program," Dean explains. "At Hopkins, I established a five-year apprenticeship program, recognized by the U.S. Bureau of Apprenticeship and Training." The preservation program became well known, and before Dean left, the conservation staff consisted of fourteen people, eleven of whom had been apprentices in the program. "While I was at the Johns Hopkins University, I obtained an M.L.A. in the history of sciences, working, as usual, at night."

Dean's current job as director of the Department of Preservation and Collection Maintenance at Cornell University began in 1985. "I moved to Cornell University to establish a new preservation program," he explains. By raising a substantial amount of money in competitive grant funding, Dean established the program and gradually built a staff of more than fifty people employed in conservation, preservation, and collection maintenance. Four conservators and three librarians are included among the staff. "In conservation," says Dean, "there are three main units: book conservation, paper conservation, and photograph conservation, and three sub-units concerned with paperback stiffening, commercial binding, and book repair."

"The essence of preservation is the maintaining of library and archival materials in usable condition," Dean explains. "Usually, conservation is regarded as caring for original materials, stabilizing them, and treating them. My tasks are to train and educate staff to carry out their duties, organize the work of the department, ensure that there are sufficient funds available, and plan and direct the work of the department. This work includes conservation, reformatting (microfilming, digital imaging, photocopying), shelving, and maintaining the collection."

The Department of Preservation and Conservation primarily serves the Cornell University Library. "Cornell has nineteen libraries and collections amounting to around nine million items," Dean says. The department operates many training programs, including one in operation for twelve years that trains conservation technicians from any library in New York State.

"Because of the work I do overseas, I regard many in other countries as my clientele," Dean adds. "In 1987, I started working in Southeast

Asia, largely because the library has the largest collection of Southeast Asian materials in the world. My work takes me to some very poor institutions throughout Southeast Asia, and I have worked in Burma, Cambodia, Laos, Thailand, Vietnam, Indonesia, Singapore, and Malaysia, spending six weeks to two months there at a time." Dean's work has also taken him to Iceland, Ireland, the United Kingdom, and France.

"Perhaps the most interesting experience was when I spent some time with the Thai Royal Princess in Bangkok discussing the conservation treatment of her music collection," says Dean. Princess Sirindorm of Thailand had attended one of Dean's presentations at an International Federation of Library Associations (IFLA) meeting in Bangkok in 1999. "A special throne was carried into the meeting room for her. Afterward, she came to me and discussed the paper, eventually asking me to come to the palace and look at her large collection of music. I did so, and made several recommendations to her. Princess Sirindorm is the most respected member of the royal family next to the king."

In his department, Dean maintains a large library of technical works including several periodicals such as *Restaurator* and the *Paper Conservator*. "It is important to have at hand a large reference collection of technical works," he says. "The department's website carries a number of opportunities for people to ask technical questions and I have to answer them all in one way or another."

Dean divides his time between his office and the various conservation facilities. He writes many grant proposals, teaches at the SUNY Albany library school and the Syracuse University library school, and conducts several workshops each year. "I have just completed a major distance learning preservation tutorial for all developing nations, beginning with Southeast Asia," he says. He is a member of IFLA, the Institute of Paper Conservation, and ALA, and usually attends their annual meetings.

Dean says that the job market in the field of preservation is fairly strong. He adds, "Librarians interested in preservation would do well to pursue the technical aspects of the profession and begin to carve out for themselves a niche within a particular library."

For more information regarding the distance learning preservation tutorial for developing nations, go to http://www.librarypreservation.org.

MELISSA A. WISNER
Library Systems Administrator
Homer Babbidge Library
University of Connecticut

Melissa A. Wisner

"What can be difficult about my job is the pressure to think three steps ahead of where the library is, while still devoting energy to where we are right now." Melissa Wisner handles this pressure well. As the library systems administrator at Homer Babbidge Library at the University of Connecticut, she is responsible for a vital part of the library's operation.

"My job is to serve as the system administrator of the integrated library system (ILS) and all of its extension modules," explains Wisner. This involves technical support of standard ILS modules such as cataloging, acquisitions, circulation, serials check-in, OPAC, custom reporting, and statistics. "I am responsible for overall system security, system maintenance, planning and managing system upgrades, troubleshooting problems with clients and servers, database cleanup and integrity, advising staff on strengths and limitations of the current ILS, serving as single source of contact with the ILS vendor, providing vision and leadership in library systems development, and working with library teams to develop the custom potential of the ILS."

Wisner is one of a twelve-member team within the library's Information Technology department. This team of library staff members is dedicated to research and development of library systems, particularly the ILS suite of products, as well as day-to-day support of the overall technological needs of the library. In addition, Wisner and her team support the library's interlibrary loan system, a suite of digital library applications including a "context-sensitive link resolver," a meta-search engine, and a digital collections management application. Wisner is involved with troubleshooting and desktop support of clients, project management for migrations, systemwide upgrades, and in-house database projects.

Wisner takes on the added obligation of developing overall leadership and vision for future library systems and being the point person for emerging trends and directions the library should undertake as they relate to library systems architecture.

"Our library expects a high return on investment from our ILS and its extension products," she explains. "I have to think about what we need to maintain service, in addition to thinking about what we expect to provide as service with each new academic year. The vitality and validity of the ILS are integral to my library's vision of success. I need to know what our ILS vendor is planning for future developments, what all ILS vendors are developing, what major IT trends will impact academic computing and therefore their relationship to the ILS, and what is standard for operating systems on desktops and servers, programming languages, and productivity software."

"Each area of the library is becoming more technology dependent," continues Wisner. "I strive to address all of their needs in a uniform and timely manner. There are days I feel overwhelmed, and I have to be strong enough to align my energy and keep moving forward."

As immersed in library systems as she is, it is a surprise that Wisner did not envision herself as a systems librarian early in her career. She knew that she wanted to become a librarian, but she saw herself involved with teaching. "Teaching was my first love, my first instinct," she says. A year after earning her undergraduate degree in English literature, she enrolled in the University of Buffalo School of Library Science in Buffalo, New York. During graduate school, she completed several strong technical internships to complement her core classes in library instruction, database searching, and cataloging.

"While in school I wasn't exactly sure what primary area of libraries I wanted to focus on," Wisner says, "but I wanted to make myself as marketable as possible to employers. I knew that meant strong technology and teaching skills." One of her internships at the University of Buffalo School of Medicine involved the development of a portal used by medical students, faculty, and community practitioners to bring together primary medical resources through one gateway. In her other internships, Wisner was given the opportunity to develop statistical report repositories to analyze collection use and other patron activity. In addition, Wisner chose to take library school courses in computer design, theories of indexing, and bibliographic instruction.

After graduating from library school, Wisner took a library teaching and technology position at the University of Connecticut School of Medicine and Dental Medicine. In that position she recognized how integral technology was to every aspect of libraries. "I wanted to be able to provide accurate, detailed answers about how databases worked, client server architecture, campus networks, authentication methodologies, and an ILS. I knew in order to gain this other insight I would need to spend some dedicated career time working from the back end of technology."

After a year as the teacher/trainer of technology, Wisner switched to the systems department for what she saw as a temporary endeavor. She found she had an aptitude for supporting technology as an administrator and ended up staying because she realized the opportunities for employment and advancement were stronger for an individual with a background and skills in systems administration. "It wasn't where I started out, or even what I thought I would do long-term in libraries," she says. "But eight years later, I'm still working in systems."

On a day-to-day basis, Wisner has a combination of task-oriented work and project-oriented work. "The task-oriented work may include setting up new operator profiles, creating a new location in the catalog, producing statistical reports, writing documentation for local use of the ILS, checking ILS server logs for any errors, or explaining the client server architecture of our ILS," she says. "The project-oriented work includes developing homegrown applications that can be used in conjunction with the ILS for general workflow efficiency, learning a program or programming language to develop these applications, or capturing some of the data in our ILS for use in other databases or applications."

"I try to make a to-do list each day, separating my work into small tasks and big projects," Wisner continues. "This is so when I feel mired down in tasks, I can look down at the list and assure myself that this isn't all I do, or when I need a break because a project is moving along on an almost evolutionary scale, I can knock off some tasks to show myself tangible proof of my workday."

Wisner finds that being on the cutting edge of technological trends and development is a big challenge. To meet this challenge head-on, she is an active member of the Library and Information Technology Association. She reads publications such as *Smart Libraries Newsletter* and ALA's *Library Technology Reports*. She monitors several electronic discussion groups, attends the annual conference of her library's ILS vendor, and is involved with NELINET, a regional library cooperative in New England. In addition, she takes continuing education courses and workshops to keep up-to-date with desktop applications or basic programming. Finally, she maintains close contact with counterparts and peers at similar organizations.

Wisner believes that it is her technical skills that have enabled her to succeed in her job. "I did begin building a foundation of technical skills in graduate school through my internships, but most of it has come from on-the-job training," she says. "I struggled with AACR2 in school, but it always pops up when supporting a MARC-based system and needing to know why an outcome is expected or unexpected. Knowing those tags and fields has helped with running queries, extracting records from our database, and improving the search interface to it. I am most grateful to one of my professors, Dr. Lorna Peterson, for reminding me to think and encouraging my abilities. I am grateful to my parents for telling me to learn how to write. All of those skills play an integral part of every day on the job. I also believe success depends on your ability to remember why you do what you do each day. If we get bogged down with too much vision or theorizing, or focus too much on just technology, we can lose sight of the basic tenets of the profession."

Wisner has some advice for those interested in systems librarianship in an academic environment. "Do what you enjoy," she says. "There will always be days when it feels like just a job, but that comes with every type of work. To make it in this profession, you need to be intelligent, outgoing, and have excellent communication skills. You need to know how to speak, write, teach, and design. You will also need project management, budgetary, personnel management, and teaming skills. It can be overwhelming, and stressful, and less than glamorous at times, but if you find an environment that is stimulating and values your skills and personal strengths, you will be satisfied." Wisner stresses that finding a healthy, professional atmosphere with a positive work environment is imperative, and that it is important to grow and develop in one's career.

"In my opinion, the job market for qualified systems staff is ideal," she says. "Employers will require that you go above and beyond the basics of the M.L.S. Be prepared to know your way around the desktop, the Internet, and standard networking configurations. You should also have at your disposal some skill with the basics such as SQL, XML/XSLT, visual basic, and some UNIX." She also says that one must be prepared to be involved in public services and to be able to make presentations to library patrons.

"Make every attempt to balance your skills while you are in graduate school and once you are working in the profession. I like to ask myself from time to time, 'If I would have to apply for the job I already have, would I still be offered it?' To make sure the answer is 'yes,' I try to stay marketable even when not actively looking for work."

"I think everyone should always strive to make the most of their time and surroundings," Wisner concludes. "The millennium provides many avenues of innovation, but this is not unique. Each decade produces innovations that eventually become standard. What is past is prologue, so it is important to remember what your main objective is in the profession, no matter where or when you find yourself."

ROBERT G. SEWELL
Associate University Librarian
for Collection Development
and Management
Rutgers University Library

Robert G. Sewell

"In this age of the hybrid library, the great challenge is to find the proper but ever-shifting balance between the new media and traditional resources." Librarian Robert Sewell must face this challenge on a daily basis. As associate university librarian for Collection Development and Management at Rutgers University, he is responsible for overseeing collection development and management in a three-campus library system located in New Brunswick, Newark, and Camden, New Jersey.

"My role is to shape the suite of collection resources available for Rutgers University Libraries, to inform faculty, students, administrators, and others about the changing nature of the economics and technologies of scholarly communications, and to advocate strongly for the enduring importance of collection development in the changing world of information and librarianship," Sewell says.

Rutgers University is a major public research institution. Its libraries' primary clientele is the university community that includes undergraduates, graduate students, administrators, professors, and advanced faculty researchers. The libraries also serve the general public. "In the last decade," says Sewell, "the three-campus libraries have developed an extremely interdependent system based on an integrated library system, a single collection budget increasingly devoted to networked electronic resources, an excellent internal document delivery system, and various systemwide policy-making groups."

Sewell is chair of the Collection Development Council, a group responsible for making collection development and management decisions involving budget and policies. "Participation at such meetings has been greatly facilitated by the recent installation of teleconferencing equipment so people from a campus sixty-five miles away can participate without having to lose most of the day in traveling," he says.

"Another feature of my position is that Special Collections and University Archives report to me. I love to jump from deciding about what electronic resources we will acquire for the system, to allocating and monitoring the collections budget, to dealing with vendors, to acquiring and conserving rare books and manuscripts, to working with donors."

Sewell finds his greatest challenge in searching for the proper balance between the acquisition of electronic resources and traditional resources such as books. "Another critical area at Rutgers is the fact that we have not yet focused enough resources on the preservation of analog material in the past," Sewell comments. "Now we are facing even more complex issues involved in the preservation or sustainability of digital resources. There are also exciting opportunities to blend traditional and digital resources in innovative ways with the use of new software, such as web research guides, EAD finding aids for manuscript and archival collections, and the digitization of analog materials."

The management of budget and time is the most difficult aspect of Sewell's job. "The exciting challenges we face come with a price tag in terms of dollars and human resources," he explains. Collections budget allocation involves particular difficulties. "In addition to funding deficiencies, the allocations may come in several stages and the total budget may not be known until well into the fiscal year, which plays havoc with budget planning. But you learn to go with the flow."

Sewell's job is not lacking in interesting experiences. One such experience involved a large collection of books found within the estate of a retired professor. The estate had been sold and the new owner wished to dispose of the books. Sewell joined a crew from the library to take a look at the book collection. "The house was a mess, but there were books everywhere," Sewell recounts. "Rickety bookshelves stuffed to the brim clogged every room on the second floor. There were unopened bags and boxes full of books throughout the house." The crew discovered that the retired professor had been an avid collector of books by the British author Walter de la Mare as well as books dealing with the occult, herbal medicine, numerology, astrology, and related topics. "There were thousands of dust-covered books from the sixteenth century to the present. No one knew that this reclusive, bachelor professor was a book collector. We had walked into a rare bibliographic gold mine. While relations with the new owner of the estate were not easy, we were able to skim the very best of the collection as a donation, but the majority was sold to a book dealer, breaking up a comprehensive research collection on the occult. This incident reflects the joys and frustrations of collection development."

Like many librarians in the field today, librarianship was not Sewell's first career choice. "I set out to become a professor of Japanese and comparative literature," he admits. He received his undergraduate degree in Asian Studies from the University of Wisconsin, an M.A. in Japanese from Columbia University, and a Ph.D. in comparative literature from the University of Illinois at Urbana-Champaign. "During my graduate studies, I began working in East Asian libraries and secured my first professional library position as Japanese bibliographer at the University of Illinois Libraries." After working in that position for several years, Sewell received his final degree, a master's in library science from Illinois. He found that librarianship was an interesting and noble career, and that if he wished to advance in his new career path, he needed that final degree.

"I worked at the University of Illinois Libraries with some of the most influential and exciting people in the field," Sewell says. "Robert Downs, the early champion for faculty status for librarians, was the dean of the libraries when I arrived." Later, under a new library administration, he worked with Hugh Atkinson and Michael Gorman, both major figures in the field because of their strong advocacy for librarians and their innovative thinking in regard to technology and management. "They created a vital atmosphere where librarians were very engaged in their local librarianship but were also professionally active, prodigious authors of scholarly work and involved in the faculty governance of the university. Professionally, it was a great place to spend my formative years in librarianship. I was given the opportunity to work as the assistant to the director of Collections and found I enjoyed collection development administration."

While at Illinois, Sewell was very active in publishing. He wrote and published fifteen articles on such topics as the history of printing in Japan, Japanese rare books and manuscripts, Japanese and comparative literature, collection development, and faculty status for librarians. "As I made my transition to administration," he says, "my pace of scholarly publication inevitably declined."

Upon leaving Illinois, Sewell worked at SUNY Stony Brook Libraries as Assistant Director of Collection Management and Development. After three years there, he accepted his current position at Rutgers University Libraries.

"My educational background has helped me relate well with faculty, students, and academic administrators, and to understand the scholarly process," says Sewell. "Many of my technical and managerial skills are self-taught, such as budgeting and statistics—subjects on which I now lecture in library school. The ability to learn on the job is essential to success in collection development or any kind of library administration."

Sewell is a member of the Association for Research Libraries and participates in workshops offered by various organizations. He is a member of the American Library Association and its Association for Library Collections and Technical Services (ALCTS). Within ALCTS, he is active in the Collection Management and Development Section, the Chief Collection Development Officers of Large Research Libraries Discussion Group, the Administration of Collection Development Committee, and the Policy and Planning Committee. He subscribes to various electronic discussion groups and "alert services" from professional publications. Finally, he reads professional literature, maintains contact with colleagues, and makes use of new technologies.

"Librarians coming into the field of collection development and management in a large academic library need a strong education background in some discipline, in addition to library and information science," Sewell says. "This provides a foundation for understanding the ways knowledge is organized and the way researchers do their work. Not only will this help in making sound collection development decisions, it also will enable the librarian to relate more effectively with students and faculty to determine their needs."

For those interested in this area of librarianship, Sewell advises, "Keep up in your subject area. At the same time, become proficient in the relevant technologies that are transforming scholarly communication. Learn the basics of budgeting, statistics, and spreadsheet software. Librarians today must deal with an increasing amount of ambiguity and change and must adhere to professional and human values within the flux. Be willing to listen closely and change as the environment changes."

SAMPLE JOB DESCRIPTIONS

Academic Reference Librarians

Environment

The primary duty of the academic reference librarian is to answer reference questions of all varieties. Since reference positions in academic libraries fall under the "public services" umbrella, many reference librarians are also given responsibility for other areas of service, such as circulation services, interlibrary loan, or instructional services. All of these areas involve direct interaction with the students, faculty, and other patrons of the institution. Reference departments vary in size from one librarian to a large team of librarians and staff members.

Responsibilities

Conduct reference interviews to determine the information needs of each patron

Notice and approach individuals who may need reference help

Utilize all available resources (print, electronic, online, telephone, etc.) to answer reference questions for patrons

Choose sources appropriate to the questions asked and to the patron's objectives and level of expertise

Suggest other support services when appropriate

Refer to colleagues for help if necessary

Keep abreast of new resources as they are added to the library collection, or as access has been provided

Instruct the patron in the use of the library's online catalog as well as other relevant databases

Establish policies and procedures for the department

Train additional reference staff in appropriate reference procedures

Participate in collection development (book and journal selection, evaluation of websites, etc.)

Participate in liaison activities with the faculty of the institution

Serve on committees within the library and institution

Engage in research, publishing, and other scholarly activities

Education and Training

A master's degree in library and information science from an ALA-accredited institution is required. Some colleges and universities also require an additional master's degree in a particular subject area of importance to the institution.

Recommended Memberships

American Library Association (ALA)

Regional and local library associations

Academic Circulation Librarians

Environment

Circulation librarians in academic libraries manage all functions of the circulation department and interact on a constant basis with library staff as well as with the patrons of the institution. Additional duties within other "public services" areas, such as interlibrary loan or reference, are often expected. Circulation departments vary in size, but usually consist of at least one librarian and a number of support staff members.

Responsibilities

Supervise all staff within the circulation department, including professional librarians, support staff, and student workers

Responsible for the scheduling and staffing of the circulation desk

Establish circulation policies and procedures

Communicate policies to patrons and staff as necessary

Coordinate training of all circulation staff in the implementation of departmental policies and procedures

Manage the circulation subsystem of the library's online catalog

Coordinate collection maintenance (shelving, weeding, shelf reading, etc.)

Manage all aspects of the interlibrary loan department

Participate in collection development (selection of books and journals)

Participate in liaison activities with the faculty of the institution

Serve on committees within the library and institution

Engage in research, publishing, and other scholarly activities

Education and Training

A master's degree in library and information science from an ALA-accredited institution is required. Some colleges and universities also require an additional master's degree in a particular subject area of importance to the institution.

Recommended Memberships
American Library Association (ALA)

Regional and local library associations

Academic Instructional Services Librarians

Environment
Instructional services librarians manage all aspects of instruction within academic libraries. Courses are generally offered to the institution's students, faculty, and staff and include instruction in: the use of the library's online catalog, searching various electronic databases, locating and evaluating websites, research skills, and so on. It is common for these librarians to have additional duties within other areas of public services, such as reference.

Responsibilities
Supervise instructional services staff

Establish and advertise courses, acting as liaison with the institution's faculty to determine which courses are needed

Prepare teaching aids, monitoring for consistency, attractiveness, and informational quality

Manage the instructional schedule

Assign the teaching of courses to various instructional services staff

Participate in active teaching

Keep library colleagues informed of program changes and equipment problems

Participate in the selection of appropriate equipment for use in teaching

Keep abreast of changes in technologies affecting course curricula

Establish a method for the evaluation of teaching and course effectiveness

Serve on committees within the library and the institution

Engage in research, publishing, and other scholarly activities

Education and Training
A master's degree in library and information science from an ALA-accredited institution is required. Some colleges and universities also require an additional master's degree in a particular subject area of importance to the institution.

Recommended Memberships

American Library Association (ALA)

Regional and local library associations

Academic Acquisitions/Serials Librarians

Environment

Acquisitions librarians in academic libraries are responsible for all the steps involved with the ordering and receipt of materials housed within the library or accessed electronically. Often, they are responsible for the acquisition of both books and journals. Acquisitions positions fall within the "technical services" area, which infers that direct contact with library patrons is limited. Today, however, many acquisitions librarians are assigned reference or circulation duties on a regular basis. Acquisitions and serials departments vary in size but generally consist of at least one librarian and a number of support staff members.

Responsibilities

Manage the budget for books and journals

Establish policies and procedures for the department

Monitor expenditures and encumbrances to ensure that funds are being expended at an appropriate rate

Oversee allocation of funds according to subject areas, academic departments, etc.

Supervise the verification, ordering, and receipt of books and journals

Train all staff in the use of the acquisitions system and in other aspects of the department

Interact with publishers and vendors on a regular basis

Provide statistical or financial reports to library administration

Maintain use statistics of both print and electronic collections

Participate in collection development (selection of books and journals for order)

Review gift materials and manage gift acknowledgments

Keep abreast of access versus ownership issues and other issues of importance, particularly concerning electronic formats

Manage all aspects of the library's electronic book and journal collection

Conduct use and cost studies to determine which journal subscriptions should be added or dropped

Solicit feedback from library users to determine changing informational needs

Participate in weeding projects

Coordinate gifts and exchange procedures

Stay abreast of new acquisitions technologies

Participate in liaison activities with the faculty of the institution

Serve on committees within the library and institution

Engage in research, publishing, and other scholarly activities

Education and Training

A master's degree in library and information science from an ALA-accredited institution is required. Some colleges and universities also require an additional master's degree in a particular subject area of importance to the institution.

Recommended Memberships

American Library Association (ALA)

North American Serials Interest Group (NASIG)

Association for Library Collections and Technical Services (ALCTS), a division of ALA

Regional and local library associations

Academic Cataloging Librarians

Environment

Academic cataloging librarians are responsible for the overall maintenance of bibliographic holdings information within the library's online public access catalog. Falling under the "technical services" umbrella, these positions involve minimal contact with library patrons. However, it is common for cataloging librarians to be assigned some reference or other public service duties. Cataloging departments vary in size from one-person operations to large groups of librarians and support staff.

Responsibilities

Supervise the input and maintenance of bibliographic information within the online catalog

Train employees in the use of all modules of the cataloging subsystem

Perform full original cataloging

Supervise copy cataloging performed by support staff

Supervise the physical processing of materials

Maintain bibliographic and authority control, ensuring the integrity of the online catalog

Maintain expert knowledge of cataloging utilities, standards, and rules

Stay abreast of changing technologies involving cataloging software, online catalogs, and cataloging in general

Prepare and provide statistical and other reports to library administration

Establish policies and procedures for the department

Participate in collection development (selection of books and journals)

Participate in liaison activities with the faculty of the institution

Serve on committees within the library and institution

Engage in research, publishing, and other scholarly activities

Education and Training

A master's degree in library and information science from an ALA-accredited institution is required. Some colleges and universities also require an additional master's degree in a particular subject area of importance to the institution.

Recommended Memberships

American Library Association (ALA)

Association for Library Collections and Technical Services (ALCTS), a division of ALA

Regional and local library associations

Academic Systems Librarians

Environment

Systems librarians in academic libraries are responsible for the administration and overall maintenance of the library's integrated library system as well as any computer-related systems or equipment used by library staff or patrons. Systems librarians must interact with library staff as well as library patrons as the need arises. Generally, library systems departments consist of one or two librarians and a varied number of support staff members.

Responsibilities

Manage and troubleshoot the library's integrated library system, including all standard modules such as cataloging, circulation, serials check-in, OPAC, interlibrary loan, and system administration

Maintain, update, and troubleshoot all computer software and equipment

Provide desktop support for library staff and patrons

Perform systemwide upgrades as required

Supervise in-house database projects

Prepare and provide statistical and other reports to library administration

Stay abreast of emerging technologies as related to library systems, the Internet, computer equipment and software, etc.

Participate in library web page development

Participate in collection development and analysis (selection of books and journals, age of collection, etc.)

Establish policies and procedures for the department

Keep staff informed of any technological or equipment changes

Participate in liaison activities with the faculty of the institution

Serve on committees within the library and institution

Engage in research, publishing, and other scholarly activities

Education and Training

A master's degree in library and information science from an ALA-accredited institution is required. A strong background in computer science or technology is recommended. Some colleges and universities also require an additional master's degree in a particular subject of importance to the institution.

Recommended Memberships

American Library Association (ALA)

Library and Information Technology Association (LITA), a division of
ALA

Regional and local library associations

Notes

1. Librarians in the Twenty-First Century: Academic Librarians, 2000, available at
   http://www.istweb.syr.edu/21stcenlib/who/academic.html. Accessed 22 October
   2002.
2. Mary Lynn Rice-Lively and J. Drew Racine, "The Role of Academic Librarians
   in the Era of Information Technology," *Journal of Academic Librarianship* 28,
   no. 1 (Jan. 1997): 31–41.
3. Robert Bleil, Academic Librarianship: Reference and Public Services, 2002,
   available at http://www.sis.pitt.edu/~lsdept/acref.htm. Accessed 22 October
   2002.

CHAPTER 4

Nontraditional Librarianship

Corporate and Freelance

Never before have there been so many opportunities in librarianship outside the traditional library setting. Historically, libraries of the past were regarded as storehouses of information, limited by physical space and defined by walls. Librarians were the keepers of knowledge, stereotyped as bespectacled elderly ladies protectively guarding the stacks while whispering "shhhh." The walls of deep-set tradition and confining stereotypes started to crumble when "PC" became an everyday acronym. At the first suggestion of something called an "information highway," the rumbles of change were more discernible. Words like "gopher" and "File Transfer Protocol" put pressure on the foundation of traditional librarianship, and cracks started to form. In no time at all, the walls came crashing down for good, thanks to the ever-changing, rapidly evolving era called the Information Age.

LIBRARIANSHIP "OUT OF THE BOX"

When the dust began to clear, librarians looked around and recognized their newfound freedom. Without buildings and walls to block their view, the horizon of opportunity stretched far and wide. They saw an abundance of information in great, disorganized heaps and recognized their niche in the business world. Always regarded as experts in the management of information and the organization of knowledge, librarians understood that this was their chance to offer their skills to a much wider variety of patrons.

It has taken a few years and more than a bit of skillful marketing, but corporations and private businesses have now come to value the unique skills possessed by those with degrees in library and information science and are more and more often finding room for information specialists and corporate librarians within their employee networks. In the private sector, librarians have had success venturing out on their own as freelance researchers, consultants, and information brokers. In an age where information seems to run the world, who is better equipped to manage, organize, and disseminate that information than those trained specifically in such skills? If information governs the world, and librarians manage information, does this mean that librarians run the world? Down deep, on the level of individual bits of knowledge, they do.

The Corporate Environment

Librarians in the business world have acquired unique titles: information specialists, knowledge managers, information architects, directors of information research, and even chief information officers (CIOs). Whatever their titles, these librarians share common charges within their organizations. In addition to locating and collecting data, they must also "evaluate, analyze, organize, package, and present information in a way that maximizes its usefulness."[1] Such individuals are often responsible for all or some of the following tasks:

the preparation of research reports;

the gathering of competitive intelligence;

the verification of facts;

the creation of databases;

the training of other employees in the use of online databases;

website creation, organization, and maintenance; and

the evaluation of software.[2]

Some, as in the case of CIOs, are involved with decision making at top management levels. Their jobs are "fast-paced, well paid, and sometimes tenuously balanced on the cutting edge."[3] As opposed to state-funded, nonprofit organizations such as public and academic libraries, most corporations and private businesses are out to make a profit. Naturally, librarians who work within these for-profit businesses tend to make more money than traditional librarians and are sometimes even offered stock options.[4] Along with higher salaries comes the turbulent, fast-paced environment common to the world of business, characterized by long hours, stressful settings, and lack of job security. For some, these factors add to the appeal of nontraditional librarianship.

Freelancing

Those valiant individuals who have ventured out on their own frequently offer the same services as corporate librarians. It is the client base that differs. Known as information brokers, library consultants, independent researchers, and informationists, these freelancers market their skills to the world at large rather than limiting their services to just one organization. Most work on their own or partner with another individual, while some work with subcontractors by farming out work to specialized researchers. Services they offer involve research (online, manual, and telephone) and document delivery. Freelance librarians usually specialize in one or more areas such as business, science, news, social science, general information, bibliographies, text, government, legislation, or public records.[5]

The success of freelance "information brokers" can in large part be attributed to the Internet. Most businesses and private individuals realize that the Internet offers a wealth of information, but they simply do not have the time, manpower, and skills to locate the information they need in the largely disorganized chaos that is the Web. Librarians can be proud of the fact that they have achieved distinction in their abilities to locate information and add value to information, and that businesses are willing to pay top dollar for these services.

SPOTLIGHTS

MARY ELLEN BATES
Principal and Information Broker
Bates Information Services

Her clients see her as a secret weapon. Marketing savvy and excellent research skills are her ammunition. Mary Ellen Bates, the principal of Bates Information Services, provides research to business professionals, backup research services to special librarians, and consulting services to the online industry. Also known as an information broker, she helps consultants, speech writers, and public relations professionals "get smart" about a company, an industry, or a technology by providing them with an information package that "lets them hit the ground running." Fortune 100 companies seek her out for in-depth research and analysis, and special librarians who have neither the required time nor the expertise pass research requests along to her. She also does consulting work for the information industry, including the professional online services, "niche" information vendors, and other companies on the Web.

"Since I'm a one-person operation, I have all the job duties of a business," says Bates. She takes on the roles of CEO, marketing vice president, sales executive, accounts payable, collections agency, administrative assistant, and researcher. For her, "there's probably no such thing as a typical day."

Without realizing it, Bates began learning how to be an entrepreneur early in her career. While pursuing her M.L.S. from the University of California, Berkeley, she took a class in special librarianship and all the programming and online research courses that were available at the time. She graduated in 1981 and worked as a corporate/special librarian for close to fifteen years.

"While I worked in special libraries, I learned how to market information services, how to do my own PC troubleshooting, how to negotiate with clients/patrons, how to conduct a reference interview, how to 'upsell' services, and how to develop new services and products as the market dictated."

After working in libraries in law firms, the federal court system, and several research companies, she got a job as library manager at MCI.

"When I started there, it was just me and a library clerk, and our mission was to serve fifteen people in the corporate planning department. Within six months after I'd started working there, I decided that I'd like to serve all 1,000 employees, and the rules at that point were, 'you can do whatever you want, so long as it doesn't cost any more money and so long as you don't make the same mistake twice.' With a mandate like that, I learned how to market the library, how to maximize every budget dollar (especially with fixed-price contracts), and how to manage my time."

Within seven years the library had grown to a staff of eight, and, weary of managing other people, Bates left the job. Having learned about information brokering from Sue Rugge, a leader in the field, she began the process of becoming an independent information professional. She joined the Association of Independent Information Professionals (AIIP).

"That was the best business decision I've ever made," she says. "I attended my first AIIP conference before I launched my business, and the experience was invaluable. I learned what to watch out for, what to expect, what mistakes everyone makes, and where to go for advice. I can't tell you how much I benefited from the experience, advice, and encouragement of more experienced members. It's a great way to meet other information brokers and expand your subcontracting network."

Bates has been an independent information professional since 1991 and still finds it remarkable that this is the longest she has ever held on to a job. She explains, "I had to laugh when I was talking with someone a few weeks ago who was interested in going into this business. I told her that I hadn't been aggravated or exasperated since I launched my business, and once I realized that, I was astonished. Yes, cash flow is a challenge and some of the day-to-day aspects of running a small company are tedious, but I love the fact that I don't have to sit in on staff meetings, I never have to ask for approval before I launch a new service or new marketing effort, and I can fire a client if he drives me crazy. There is so much that I like about being an independent information professional—the flexibility to try new things, the satisfaction of running my own business, and the freedom to define my job and my responsibilities."

Bates has plenty of advice for anyone thinking of pursuing a career as an independent information professional. "You either have to be an excellent researcher yourself or be able to subcontract the research to other excellent researchers. You need a strong background as an online searcher using the professional online services, or a strong background in a specialized area of research such as public records research or telephone research."

"The hardest part of this profession is running a business," she says. She recommends taking classes on entrepreneurship and business such as accounting, marketing, and sales. "As much as you love research, information brokering also involves a lot of nitty-gritty business skills."

Before setting up a business, it helps to have research expertise in a subject area as well as personal name recognition within some segment of the target industry. Influential contacts are helpful as well. "Almost all your business will be from word of mouth, and you only get that from satisfied customers. This isn't the kind of profession you can learn on the job. There's very little room for error."

Bates is blunt when she says, "It's not a business where you'll get rich quick. Expect 50–60 hour workweeks. Expect to market like crazy the first couple of years and to spend at least 30 percent of your time marketing after that. The first year will be a lean year, income-wise."

It may not be an easy career move, but "it's a very gratifying and exciting career in that you make your own opportunities."

"If you're good," says Bates, "the sky's the limit."

In addition to running her business, Mary Ellen Bates speaks frequently on topics related to the information industry. She is also a writer and has written or co-authored five books and one professional white paper. Her most recent work is titled *Building and Running a Successful Research Business: A Guide for the Independent Information Professional*, published by Information Today. Her website (http://www.BatesInfo.com) features a "Tip of the Month" with useful discussion on issues relevant to independent information professionals.

George Soete

GEORGE SOETE
Organizational Development Consultant
Specializing in Libraries

"Consulting is allied to librarianship in at least one important respect: it is a helping profession. . . . If you are not interested in helping others, you should probably not waste your time being a consultant."

By enabling them to plan, solve problems, and become better organizations, George Soete is the ultimate "helper" of libraries. In his role as organizational development consultant, he offers "process consulting" services, so named because he helps people through processes rather than advising them on technical issues. He is most often hired by academic libraries to do consulting, training, or writing. His consulting jobs have involved strategic planning, team building, and organizational diagnosis. He has offered training in communication, conflict management, process improvement, project planning, customer service, and team concepts. Commonly, he works with a "leadership group" consisting of five to twenty administrators and department heads, but on pleasurable experiences in organizations have been when I've been able to work with all staff, at least in information or training sessions," he says.

Soete has not always been a freelance consultant. "First, the facts," he says. "I am a librarian." After earning his M.L.S. degree from the University of Wisconsin, Soete served as reference librarian, head of collections, and administrator in several different public and academic libraries. He completed the ARL Consultant Training Program and subsequently attended several intensive workshops to supplement his skills, including training in the Myers-Briggs Type Indicator, Experiential Learning Skills, Organizational Development, Organizational Change, and Group Facilitation. It seems the steps he took in his career served to strengthen his skills as a consultant.

"One of the delightful things that happens when you get older," he says, "is that you begin to see that just about everything you've done in your life has prepared you to be where you are today."

Soete started consulting and training in 1979, while working as a library administrator at the University of California, San Diego. "When I took early retirement in 1993, I was really shifting careers—doing full-time what I had been doing part-time for fourteen years."

Now Soete has the privilege of interacting with libraries from an alternative perspective. Having learned the ropes by working as a librarian himself, he is uniquely qualified to help libraries improve in a variety of ways. "On my best days," he says, "I feel that I have an important role in helping libraries become better at what they do and contribute more effectively to the information community."

His work has allowed for some interesting observations. "My clients are obviously smart, accomplished people. This is a tremendous benefit," he says. Then he adds, "but also a drawback sometimes." He goes on to explain that often smart, competent people can have a difficult time observing their own behavior, learning from what they observe, and changing to meet the needs of a changing environment. Librarians, in particular, "are quite cerebral people." Soete finds this to be a wonderful characteristic but also a challenging one. "They enjoy theoretical discussions and they like to explore issues on a hypothetical level," he explains. "It can sometimes, however, be difficult for them to follow through with actions. Helping libraries through action planning is one of the most challenging jobs I have."

Equally interesting to Soete is the organizational culture of the libraries that hire him. After working a bit within an organization, he can usually spot cultural characteristics. "There are cultures of energy, cultures of achievement, cultures of risk-taking, cultures of teamwork, cultures of complaint, cultures of blame, and so forth. What's interesting about organizations is that these cultures are quite persistent. People come and go, and unless there is deliberate and pervasive change, the culture will change very little. In any consultation, I try to help organizations make at least tiny incremental changes."

Soete finds the tremendous variety in his work to be exciting and unique. His days are anything but routine. Whether working on-site for a client, traveling to a client site, or working from his home office, he remains disciplined and focused on his work. "When so much of your time is discretionary, as it is for consultants," he explains, "you absolutely must be a disciplined self-starter. It helps that I have a strong inner control—I am profoundly unhappy when my work isn't finished." Soete does confess to some down time on occasion, particularly on airplanes where he reads newspapers, "trashy mysteries," or listens to CDs.

"It's been truly wonderful having two very different serial careers: librarianship and consulting," says Soete. "Viewing library organizations as a consultant, from the outside, has provided me with many insights about how people work together, how they lead, how they fight, and how they dream."

He credits the success of his career to the people at the Office of Management Services at ARL, who provided him with training and support. "I would not have had a consulting career without them."

For anyone interested in becoming a freelance consultant for libraries, Soete wants to make it clear that such a job is not easy. "We know how ridiculous it is when we hear someone say, 'anyone can teach.' We also know that it requires intensive training and experience to become an effective librarian. Well, the same is true of consulting. It takes more than knowledge of a technical area such as library automation to be a good consultant. It would appear on the surface that the central act of consulting is giving advice. Yet although good consultants sometimes do give advice, the best ones spend much more time listening to the client, gathering data, coaching the client through planning and decision processes. A good consultant is first a good listener."

"Perhaps the best advice, then, is take it seriously," says Soete. "Get some training. Learn to listen as you've never listened before. Work hard. Be generous. Respect the fact that your clients are the only ones who can really solve their problems and that you are there not so much as a repository of wisdom but as a facilitator, a true helper."

In addition to his freelance work, George Soete often writes for the Association of Research Libraries (ARL) and for other clients. He also teaches library and information science courses for the San Jose State University Library School. To learn more about George Soete and the services he offers, visit his website at http://www.georgesoete.com.

CINDY ALTICK CUNNINGHAM
U.S. Catalog Librarian
Amazon.com

In her role at Amazon.com, Cindy Altick Cunningham brings cataloging to a new level by using words and codes to market products online. As catalog librarian, her main goal is to understand the various data elements that enable customers to find what they want easily. "I

Cindy Altick Cunningham

am trying to guarantee a positive customer experience by allowing people to find and identify the item they're seeking," she says.

Linking cataloging to marketing is not as long a stretch as it may seem. Librarians have long been in the business of helping patrons find the books they want or need. Cunningham's interest in cataloging data is based on traditional cataloging philosophy: describe physical things so they can be found easily and then be linked to related items. In the business world, especially when the Internet is involved, this formula has rapidly become one of the keys to successful marketing.

"It has been an interesting experience to watch as Amazon's demand for cataloging data in order to sell items has led industries like toys and tools to consider how to put more attention into the data record itself and to understand how powerful good data is as a marketing tool," says Cunningham. "Having the chance to work with vendors and watch this change in the marketplace as a result of Amazon's influence has been exciting."

Librarianship was not Cunningham's initial career choice. With an undergraduate degree in international relations from Stanford University, she was a community journalist for five years. After enrolling in Washington's Graduate School of Library and Information Science, she participated in a National Science Foundation grant on artificial intelligence. "This background helped me immeasurably to understand computer/data behavior and end-users."

As a professional librarian, Cunningham worked in a variety of academic and public libraries, including the Library of Congress, University of Washington, and Kitsap Regional Library. She was recruited by Amazon.com in 1998.

Cunningham interacts with a variety of people in her day-to-day job. She serves publishers and industry professionals in the outside community, primarily working with software engineers and business development colleagues. Much of her time is spent answering queries from other companies regarding the status of data they have sent and how to improve or change it. Inside the company, she answers questions about the work of the engineering team she supports, whose projects include companywide initiatives and business team initiatives. "I work closely with a team of engineering managers to understand their priorities, project status, and resource constraints."

"I am seen by many as a bridge between libraries and the kinds of changes that e-commerce has brought," says Cunningham. She stays on top of the changes that occur in the marketplace by attending conferences and meetings, serving on committees outside the company, and by staying in close touch with contacts at other businesses.

She also attends library-related conferences to keep up with library issues. "Librarians have a valuable skill set, as information seekers, as mediators between those seeking information and the information itself, as designers of information," she explains. "We should not lose sight of how much we still bring to any situation. We must remain open to the changing nature of our profession, of our institutions, and of the power shifts between who has information, who is viewed as an expert, and who will pay for information. We need to be flexible and creative and willing to take risks to see that the right decisions are made and that information have-nots are served."

To those interested in an e-commerce career, Cunningham says the need for those with library and database-building skills can be found in unexpected places. "Be creative about where you apply to work," she says. Certain skills, such as cataloging, database construction, searching, indexing, and other technical skills are a plus in an online environment.

"Working in e-commerce can open your eyes and give you, as a librarian, a chance to make a real difference. Don't be afraid to take risks, if what you're after is experience! You'll never be disappointed, and you may have some good stories to tell later."

Cunningham is enthusiastic about the library profession. "I can't imagine a better education to have in this information-saturated world," she says. "I think anything a librarian does, from a traditional setting to something very unusual, is valuable and serves the world in valuable ways. Librarians shouldn't be afraid to try something very different, and to take risks."

SUSAN M. KLOPPER
Director
Business Research Center
Arthur Andersen LLP

What does it mean to be a librarian in this new millennium? Susan Klopper, a librarian at Arthur Andersen, responds, "It means that you are not afraid to find and use your voice to let it be known that you and your team are direct contributors to your organization's mission and

Susan M. Klopper

customers. It means that you are willing to take risks and put yourself on the line to demonstrate accountability and innovative thinking. It means that you are too busy planning ahead and wowing your organization to be sidelined by the 'L' word."

As director of Arthur Andersen's Business Research Center, Klopper certainly practices what she preaches by taking risks and putting herself on the line on a regular basis. She is responsible for managing a team that provides a range of support services to the consulting, tax, and audit operations of the firm. The team's primary internal clients are the twelve practices located in various cities within the southeastern United States. Outside clients include global industry groups. Most of the individuals served by Business Research Center are CPAs, attorneys, engineers, and MBAs.

Klopper works for an organization "whose very survival is dependent on its ability to understand and meet the complex business needs of its clients." This environment challenges her to create innovative and responsive products and services that speak to her clients' information needs and that support the organization's bottom line. "In other words," she explains, "by taking my cues from my organization, I have learned what my job is really all about: to contribute to the success of my company. The excitement and intensity of meeting that challenge is extraordinary, and it provides me with opportunities to shine as a librarian every single day."

Klopper's job description contains an extensive list of responsibilities, including directorship of the research center, management of budgets, collection development and organization, mentorship of other employees, complex research and analysis, contract negotiation, the conducting of information audits and surveys, and the creation and implementation of learning programs for information access. "As for a day-to-day routine," she says, "just take all of those responsibilities and throw them up in the air. As they hit the ground, that is what I might be doing at any particular moment in time." In addition to her hectic everyday projects, she devotes time to professional organizations such as the Special Libraries Association (SLA), where she currently serves on the board of directors, the American Association of Law Libraries (AALL), and the Atlanta Law Libraries Association (ALLA). She frequently speaks at international information conferences on topics related to business research, information management, and leadership, and she regularly writes articles for industry trade journals such as *Online, Business Information Alert,* and *Searcher.* She keeps up with technology by subscribing to library-specific and general technology magazines and by participating in a number of electronic discussion groups. She has also learned the value of communicating with vendors and being willing to provide critical analysis of products and services. "I jump at opportunities to test run, tweak, and compare as many products as I can," she explains. "It is my job, my responsibility, and my security. I might also add that it's great fun!"

With an undergraduate degree in art history, Klopper's first career was in museum curatorial work, a field she pursued for about ten years before switching to librarianship. "Believe it or not, one of the reasons that I became a librarian was to make more money. A friend of mine who was attending library school at Southern Connecticut gave me a tour of the school. The first thing I saw was a room filled with computers. Bells went off. Here was my chance to keep both feet firmly planted in the humanities while learning some marketable skills." While in library school at Southern Connecticut State University, Klopper decided to focus on employment in a corporate library. She completed two internships, one in a telephone company and another in a medical hospital library. Her experience in the hospital library set the tone for the direction her career would take. The head librarian there taught her that "the customer was king and the most important service we could provide was exceptional quality work that both supported and anticipated the customer's information needs." Her tedious, time-consuming work with print indexes taught Klopper the value of quality assurance.

"My other useful lessons came from my days working in the museum. The staff was small and so I was a jack-of-all-trades. That taught me that not only was I good at multitasking, but that I thrived on it. I also had to spend a fair amount of time thinking of creative ways to 'sell' my program ideas to the museum's board of directors. I'm not sure if I appreciated it at the time, but these experiences have come in use every single day that I have worked in my organization."

For those interested in a career in a corporate environment, Klopper recommends taking a few business, accounting, and management classes. "Be prepared to learn the jargon, the culture, the mission, and the businesses" of any organization of interest. "You will also need to be prepared to market and sell your products and services to your clients and to develop business plans to justify and implement new programs."

Klopper says that certain "librarian" skills that are helpful in the corporate world include the ability to understand how information is organized, the capacity to tap into and develop strong networks, and propensity to engender trust. "There are many other skills that have been instrumental to my success: a curious and interested nature, strong bent toward marketing, a stubborn streak which prevents me from giving up, knowledge of financial statements, and persuasive verbal and written communication skills."

"Be excited and passionate about your work," says Klopper. "Be willing to work very hard, and make sure that 'innovation' is an everyday part of your vocabulary. Lose these qualities and you lose your edge."

"Oh, and about all that library image baggage which we have traditionally dragged around with us—leave it at home."

JOANN M. WLEKLINSKI
Knowledge Management Manager
Technology Awareness Group
Accenture Technology Labs

Joann M. Wleklinski

"I read and write for my living." Sounds like a librarian's dream. But Joann Wleklinski's job is a far cry from that of your average librarian. As knowledge management manager in the Technology Awareness Group at Accenture Technology Labs, her job is to "write about what the analysts are saying about technology."

The Technology Awareness Group (TAG) consists of five writers who produce three technology newsletters—two for internal distribution at Accenture and one for external distribution outside the firm. Wleklinski is one of those writers.

"I am the editor of *Viscera: The Journal of Technology Prognostication*," she explains. "*Viscera* reports on what analysts are saying about a particular technology. *Viscera* focuses on the future—what the analysts are predicting will happen with a given technology, say, three to five years out."

"*Viscera*'s primary audience is Accenture consultants—technology-savvy people who are often too busy to read all that there is to read on a subject. *Viscera* provides them with a sort of 'Cliffs Notes' on currently popular technology topics, and what the outlook for those technologies is."

Wleklinski has a B.A. in English and an M.L.I.S. from Rosary College (now known as Dominican University). "I also have a chef's degree with further study done in the south of France with Simone Beck," she says as an aside. After receiving her library degree, she served at the United Nations on a three-month temporary assignment. Soon after that, she was hired by Andersen Consulting, which is now known as Accenture. Her work there began in the research library where she supported the information needs of the company's researchers. Eventually she was hired into her current position by TAG, located two floors above the library. When asked, "how did you end up where you are today?" she glibly replies, "the elevator."

It took some time for Wleklinski to select library and information science as a career. "I was interested in so many things, I couldn't pick any one thing," she explains. "That's what led me to library school—libraries cover all the subjects, right? Once in library school, I realized I'm an information geek at heart. It doesn't matter what the subject is. As long as I'm ferreting out information about anything, I'm happy."

Not only do information and technology keep her happy, they also present Wleklinski with exciting challenges. "The most challenging feature of my job is keeping ahead of the curve on interesting technology topics to report on," she says. Changing technology is at the heart of her job, and she keeps up by attending research seminars at Accenture Technology Labs and by reading everything she can get her hands on, including newspapers, magazines, reports, and web publications. She also attends analyst seminars and conferences to maintain contacts in the industry and keeps an eye out for topics of interest within the Special Libraries Association.

"My audience is pretty sophisticated and well-versed in technology. Staying abreast, if not ahead of them, is my challenge. It's also the most exciting part of my job. I thrive on 'what's the buzz?' and 'what's new?'"

"In the world of digital information, so much is changing—and changing rapidly," she says. "Issues of copyright. Availability of broadband. The world of digital distribution. It surely is a very exciting time to be involved in the world of information and delivery."

Wleklinski shares a bit of career advice when she says, "Get to know thyself. Figure out what you love to do. Then figure out a way to do what you love to do. Network with as many people as you can. Establish relationships, so that you can then do what you love to do."

LOUIS ROSENFELD
Principal and Information Architect
Louis Rosenfeld LLC
Information Architecture Consulting

Imagine finding an aesthetically pleasing website full of wonderful content, but you are unable to find the information you need. You know it's there. You are frustrated beyond measure. When you do manage to stumble across it, you print out the pages for fear of never finding them again. The website is in desperate need of help.

Enter Louis Rosenfeld. As a freelance information architect, his job is to design and improve information systems with the ultimate goal of enabling people to find information efficiently. Using the above scenario, the company that created the website would hire Rosenfeld as a consultant, assigning him the task of "fixing" things so that the website's valuable content could be found easily.

"The dry definition of information architecture," says Rosenfeld, "is 'the art and science of structuring, organizing, and labeling information so users can search and browse it more effectively, and so owners can manage it more effectively.' It's an emerging field with thousands of practitioners who apply techniques and methods drawn from established fields to design and improve information systems. Naturally, most of these systems are web-based and are developed in a business context."

Rosenfeld received his M.I.L.S. from the University of Michigan's School of Information and Library Studies. "I was interested in databases and naively figured that ILS was a nice middle ground between computer science and getting an MBA," he says. After a few library-related jobs, he returned to the school and completed two years of doctoral work, where he had the opportunity to teach and do research. He also worked in three University of Michigan libraries.

Despite these experiences, Rosenfeld never saw himself becoming a professor, nor did he plan on becoming a traditional librarian. What was he looking for? "I wasn't really sure," he explains, "but with the IT revolution exploding all over the place, it was clear that librarianship was only going to grow in importance. After all, who'd organize all the huge volumes of information the world was about to create? I didn't exactly know which non-library venue I'd end up in, but then along came the Web."

For ten years Rosenfeld was president of Argus Associates, a company that exclusively provided information architecture consulting and design services. Clients included Fortune 500 companies such as Microsoft, AT&T, and Daimler Chrysler. "Now I'm a solo consultant. My recent clients include Hewlett-Packard and Ford."

Rosenfeld also provides information architecture training at numerous conferences. "I find that the best way to learn new material is to try to teach or write about it."

When he was in library school, there were no courses offered on information architecture. Things have changed since then. "I'm both excited and jealous to report that today there are many courses, tracks, and even a few full programs in information architecture," says Rosenfeld. However, he is quick to point out that traditional librarianship courses are still valuable and necessary.

"Whenever someone in or just about to enter library school asks me what courses they should take, I think they expect me to recommend a few programming classes. I never do. Reference and cataloging are absolutely the most important things you can learn at library school. Just be sure to take them with a grain of salt. See them as opportunities to learn important principles that can be ported to multiple environments, not just traditional ones."

To those interested in a career in information architecture, Rosenfeld says that the job market is extremely tough. "This means that new information architects will have to create their own positions. In turn, that means being highly entrepreneurial, something that not many people are very good at doing, especially those with LIS backgrounds."

Once employed, he suggests that "it's good to be able to 'speak' the language of your colleagues, be they programmers or others. But good heavens, that doesn't mean you have to *become* them! The best design takes place in an interdisciplinary environment; bring your LIS brain to that setting, and be prepared to communicate with colleagues who come from entirely different backgrounds."

What does it mean to be a librarian in this new millennium? To Rosenfeld, it means "recognizing that librarianship is and must be portable, and that its principles are applicable to any information medium and in any venue. Practitioners absolutely have to be able to envision themselves plying and advocating their trade outside traditional formats (i.e., books) and settings (i.e., libraries). Otherwise there eventually will be no librarians in the new millennium."

For more information about Louis Rosenfeld and the services he offers, visit his website at http://louisrosenfeld.com.

PAMELA ANDERSON KERNS
Northeast Sales Coordinator
Majors Scientific Books

Pamela Anderson Kerns

"Have MLS—Will Travel." This was the heading of a classified ad placed by a medical book distributor in 1979. The company wanted a librarian to work with their library accounts, publish their newsletter, and manage the approval and continuation programs. The unusual ad caught the eye of librarian Pam Kerns, whose experience had always been in health sciences libraries. When offered the position, she accepted it. "The rest is history," she says.

For the past fourteen years, Kerns has been working for Majors Scientific Books as their Northeast Sales Coordinator. In this position, Kerns offers collection development options to health sciences librarians, medical bookstores, and college bookstores in the northeast. "I see my role as a teacher, facilitator, and translator; the middle person between the library or bookstore and Majors. My job is to offer options and opportunities and provide solutions built around Majors Scientific Books' services," she says. In addition, she relays the needs of the libraries back to Majors. "This enables Majors to create new services, pursue new publishers, and be aware of new technologies and trends." Her primary clientele are technical services professionals and staff members, particularly ones dealing with book selection and continuations. She also visits procurement or purchasing agents.

"There is not a standard day-to-day routine. This is the most interesting part of the work," says Kerns, who works out of her apartment in Brooklyn. "A day could be spent on the computer, planning sales trips, talking to accounts, or answering accounts' questions or concerns." As the ad for her first job with a vendor promised twenty years ago, Kerns also spends a lot of time on the road. "Even though travel can be trying at times, it still has offered me the chance to visit many different areas and to meet many wonderful people."

Kerns earned her M.L.S. from the University of Maryland. A few years later, she took night courses and completed a master's program in public administration from Baruch College of the City University of New York. The program offered courses in planning, budgeting, administration, and health care, and guided her toward an understanding of health-care issues beyond medical education and acute care. "It offered the opportunity to see medical information go full circle—need, research, medical education, acute care, long-term care, and the planning and financial concerns that go with each step."

Armed with her degrees and her knowledge of libraries, Kerns was well qualified for her job, but admits to the necessity of some on-the-job training. "To me, learning is a lifelong activity," she explains. "I brought my library knowledge and applied it to a different location in the information process. If one considers information management as a process, then book distribution is simply a part of that process." Recently, her clientele expanded to health science bookstores. She considers this new learning experience, "the art of book selling," an adventure.

Kerns keeps up with changing technology and with the world of librarianship through her membership in the Medical Library Association and all its regional chapters within her sales territory. She serves on committees and attends annual meetings, where she has the opportunity to talk with clientele and visit with other vendors.

"'Flexibility' is the one word that could sum up any advice I could give," says Kerns. "I think this also describes librarians and information management in the new millennium. The skills one learns can be applied to many fields—book publishing, book selling, or journal subscription agencies. Journals or books in electronic format also offer possible careers outside the traditional library setting. Database companies as well as integrated library systems are other wonderful options."

Kerns truly enjoys working in such a unique capacity with other professional librarians. "To provide information, services, or training to members of one's own profession," she says, "is a wonderful job."

SAMPLE JOB DESCRIPTIONS

Freelance Information Brokers (Informationists, Information Consultants, and Independent Researchers)

Environment

Information brokers offer in-depth research services to businesses and individuals. They commonly work independently and own and manage their own businesses.

Responsibilities

Perform online, manual, or telephone research for clients by set deadlines

Locate, analyze, and interpret information and data by set deadlines (often involves specialization in one or more areas of research such as business, science, news, legislation, general information, etc.)

Offer document delivery

Market the business (requires entrepreneurial skills and marketing savvy)

Manage the accounting and fee collection aspects of the business

Education and Training

Normally requires a master's degree in library and information science from an ALA-accredited institution. Experience working in libraries (particularly as a reference librarian) is recommended. An advanced degree in another area such as law or business is recommended but not required. Specialized training in online research, entrepreneurship, marketing, negotiation, and PC troubleshooting is strongly recommended.

Recommended Memberships

Special Libraries Association (SLA)

Association of Independent Information Professionals (AIIP)

Freelance Library Consultants

Environment

Freelance consultants specializing in libraries offer a variety of services to libraries, from strategic planning to group facilitation. Most work independently and own and manage their own businesses.

Responsibilities

Assist libraries with long-range strategic planning

Offer recommendations for improvement of floor plans and library layouts

Observe and analyze library organization and management; offer recommendations for improvement

Offer training in communication, group facilitation, conflict management, project planning, customer service, and team building (requires the ability to engender trust and to motivate people)

Market the business (requires entrepreneurial skills and marketing savvy)

Manage the accounting and fee collection aspects of the business

Education and Training

A master's degree in library and information science from an ALA-accredited institution is the norm. Experience working in libraries, particularly as an administrator, is recommended. An advanced degree in another area such as business is recommended but not required. Specialized training in consulting, experiential learning, organizational development, change management, library architecture, and group facilitation is strongly recommended.

Recommended Memberships

Special Libraries Association (SLA)

Association of Research Libraries (ARL)

Association of Independent Information Professionals (AIIP)

Corporate Librarians (Chief Information Officers, Knowledge Managers, Chief Answerists, and Information Specialists)

Environment

Corporate librarians generally provide research and information services to employees within for-profit organizations. Depending on the size of the company, they may work independently or as part of a team.

Responsibilities

Provide in-depth research to all employees within the organization

Conduct competitive intelligence regarding products, services, and strategies at competing organizations (requires in-depth knowledge of the business industry)

Manage collection budgets

Collection development and organization

Supervise the purchasing of materials

Prepare reports

Manage and train "library" employees

Train employees of the organization in the use of online databases and other information sources

Consult on knowledge management, web page development, and database design

Education and Training

A master's degree in library and information science from an ALA-accredited institution is usually required. An additional degree in an area such as business is common. Specialized training in commerce, marketing, accounting, and management is strongly recommended.

Recommended Memberships

Special Libraries Association (SLA)

Associations specific to the organization's area of business (such as the American Association of Law Libraries)

Information Architects

Environment

Information architects design various systems to help users access and manage different types of information. The information architect's goal is to minimize the time users spend searching or browsing for information, usually in the context of a website. They may work independently as consultants, or as specialists within organizations.

Responsibilities

Design various systems (search systems, labeling systems, navigation systems, organization systems, etc.) that allow people to find information successfully

Maintain in-depth, up-to-date knowledge of the organization of information, information systems, technology, information retrieval, and user interfaces for various systems

Explore the needs of the organization to create the most appropriate information architecture

Market the business (if freelance, requires entrepreneurial skills and marketing savvy)

Manage the accounting and fee collection aspects of the business (if freelance)

Education and Training

A master's degree in library and information science from an ALA-accredited institution is usually required. Some experience with or specialized training in cataloging, metadata, web page design, or database design is strongly recommended.

Recommended Memberships

Special Libraries Association (SLA)

American Society for Information Science and Technology (ASIST)

Notes

1. Special Libraries Association, Special Librarians Putting Knowledge to Work, 2002, available at http://www.sla.org/content/SLA/professional/meaning/what/index.cfm. Accessed 10 May 2002.
2. Ibid.
3. Margaret Thomas, "Crossing Over . . . to the Corporate Sector," *Library Journal* 126 (Sept. 1, 2001): 48–50.
4. Ibid.
5. Brenda C. Rosen, "The Age of the Information Broker: An Introduction," *Reference Librarian* 22 (1988): 5–16.

CHAPTER 5

Medical and
Law Librarianship

The basic role of the medical librarian and the law librarian is identical to that of librarians in general: to collect information and organize it for effective use.[1] Subject specialty is what differentiates these two fields of librarianship from others. For this reason, these two disciplines often fall within the realm of "special librarianship." Specialized education and training, vocabulary specific to law or medicine, and a working relationship with professionals in the fields of law or medicine make these two areas of librarianship unique.

MEDICAL LIBRARIANSHIP

Imagine having a hand in saving a person's life by performing a literature search. Imagine designing a website to help people find information about their health, such as cancer or heart disease or diabetes. Imagine helping to care for animals by determining their proper nutritional requirements. Imagine assisting in the architectural design of a zoo. Imagine training medical students to use specialized databases so that they may find relevant medical information when they become doctors. Although these experiences may sound remarkable and unlikely, they are common occurrences for those working within the various specialties of medical librarianship.

Also called health sciences librarians, medical librarians work in a variety of settings: hospitals, clinics, medical schools, consumer health centers, academic health centers, government agencies, Internet companies, pharmaceutical manufacturers, research centers, veterinary hospitals, and even zoos. Wherever there is a need for health information, there is a niche for a medical librarian. This diversity in medical librarianship is a fairly recent notion in the context of librarianship in general. Although medical "libraries" were known to be in existence for centuries, the idea of the specialized medical librarian did not truly take shape until the founding of the Medical Library Association in 1898.[2] Even after that, the concept of a separate health sciences library run by a specially trained librarian took some time to take root. Throughout the first half of the twentieth century, the profession gradually but steadfastly spread its shoots and feelers until it had successfully made its way into the heart of the health information industry.

Today opportunities in medical librarianship abound. The growth of both information technology and the healthcare industry has contributed to an explosion of health information. The U.S. healthcare environment, in particular, now puts great emphasis on consumer and patient health education. As a result, medical librarians not only serve healthcare professionals, they now also work to provide health information—through hospitals, academic medical libraries, special consumer health centers, or community service agencies—to healthcare consumers.[3] The abundance of health-related information on the Internet has obliged medical librarians to develop expertise in searching the Web for health information, and then sorting the good from the bad.

Positions in medical librarianship vary widely depending on the work environment. Academic medical librarians, for example, most often work with medical students and medical school faculty, and may be involved in medical reference, Internet services, Web management, instruction, cataloging, collection development, serials management, or administration. Hospital librarians, also called clinical librarians, provide medical information services and instruction to physicians, nurses, allied health professionals, and patients, and may also be involved with administration and technical services. Samples of job titles within the realm of medical librarianship include medical reference librarian, information services librarian, digital archivist, Web manager, electronic resources coordinator, collection development officer, cataloger, serials librarian, circulation librarian, instructor, medical library director, clinical librarian, pharmaceutical librarian, bioinformatics specialist, veterinary librarian, and zoo librarian.

Despite the variety of job titles, medical librarians share many professional interests, including changing medical technologies, delivery of health care, medical terminology, healthcare information on the Internet, institutional accreditation, and medical and professional ethics. They also share the satisfaction of filling a valuable and indispensable role within the health information industry.

LAW LIBRARIANSHIP

"Law librarianship is characterized by variety."[4] Though most law librarians specialize in finding and organizing legal information, the environments in which they work vary widely. Many organizations, including law schools, private law firms, and government agencies, have found real value in recruiting librarians to help handle the endless amounts of information associated with the world of law.

Specific duties of law librarians vary according to the type and size of the library in which they are employed. They may be involved in public services, cataloging, collection development, reference services, or, in the case of a small library, they may be involved in all of these areas. The library's primary clientele also plays a big part in determining the law librarian's responsibilities. Librarians in law firms or private corporations, for example, generally consider attorneys as their primary patrons and assist them with various levels of research. Academic law librarians provide research assistance to the students and faculty of a university's school of law. Court librarians help judges or lawyers locate information related to particular cases being tried at that court. Prison law librarians serve the legal information needs of prison inmates.

Many law librarians have had previous experience in the field of law, either as attorneys, as legal aides, or in some other legal capacity. For this reason, it is a common misconception that a law librarian must have a law degree in addition to a degree in librarianship. In fact, less than 20 percent of law librarian jobs require both degrees.[5] There is generally no law degree requirement for librarian positions in private firms or government law libraries. However, a law degree is usually required for reference librarians in law schools as well as for directors of academic law libraries. It is interesting to note that, while a degree in librarianship alone will open doors to all kinds of careers in law libraries, a law degree alone will rarely qualify for the same opportunities. Obviously, professionals in the legal world have recognized and accepted the need for trained, specialized librarians to organize and retrieve legal information.

SPOTLIGHTS

Stewart Brower

STEWART BROWER
Coordinator
Information Management Education
University at Buffalo
Health Sciences Library

"I see my role as split between being an educator and a problem-solver." As coordinator of Information Management Education at the University at Buffalo (UB) Health Sciences Library (HSL), Stewart Brower has the opportunity to exercise his teaching and reference skills on a daily basis. His job is to coordinate the library's educational programs, which include workshops and course-based instruction. He teaches a good number of those workshops and classes, is involved with reference duties, runs bibliographic searches, and helps train student employees.

"I also have a liaison appointment to UB's School of Pharmacy, where I participate in faculty committees, work on curriculum integration of information skills training, and select books and other materials for their area," says Brower. "Add to this that I'm tenure-track and working on publications, and I keep plenty busy."

For Brower, the wide variety of patrons served makes working in an academic health sciences library a unique experience. "Not only do we have students at both the undergraduate and graduate levels and researchers and teaching faculty, but we're also open to the public," he explains. "Sometimes we're helping out laypeople, whose friends or family members are sick and need some information. Occasionally we get lawyers or private researchers who have more complex information needs. Once in a while, high school students who need assistance with a school paper will come in."

The diversity of tasks and duties, which vary from day to day, is also appealing to Brower. "I can't imagine having a routine," he says. During the fall semester, he generally teaches one class or workshop per day, but has been known to teach as many as three. "I really love to teach, whether in the classroom or at the reference desk. I enjoy finding ways to explain difficult concepts so that very different kinds of learners all still walk away with the knowledge they need. It can be challenging, but the rewards can be amazing too."

When he's not teaching, Brower is often preparing for a class by developing class materials and examples, creating library-based assignments, or drafting handouts. He reads articles and books and takes classes to improve his instructional methods. Daily meetings—including reference staff meetings, space planning meetings, faculty meetings, curriculum committee meetings, and impromptu meetings with colleagues—occupy much of his time. "I also spend a great deal of time e-mailing or on the phone—scheduling meetings or class times with other HSL instructors, or confirming audiovisual setups for specific classes, or checking availability of classroom space."

In addition, Brower spends some hours staffing the reference desk and wishes he could afford to spend more time there. "I don't think anything really gives librarian[s] better experience with the information behaviors of their clientele more than sitting reference." Finally, with what little time he has remaining, Brower does some collection development for pharmacy and pharmaceutics, works on professional development and association and committee work, and tries to do some professional writing for publication. Admitting that he finds time management the most difficult aspect of his job, Brower says, "There are just not enough hours in the day to get done everything that needs to be done."

Brower stumbled upon a career in health sciences librarianship a bit by chance. While working on his undergraduate degree in English at Oklahoma State University, he landed a work-study position in one of the university's libraries. After graduating with his B.A., he was hired by the library as a serials clerk. Influenced by some of his librarian co-workers, he soon realized that the thought of becoming a professional librarian appealed to him. He enrolled in the master's program in library and information studies at the University of Oklahoma. While in library school, he not only met his future wife, he also gained valuable experience by working in a regional hospital library.

After graduating with his master's, Brower spent six "golden years" working as a professional librarian at the Oklahoma University Health Sciences Library. Then, falling victims to wanderlust, he and his wife moved to St. Louis where he worked as technology development and promotions librarian at Washington University's medical library. "I fine-tuned my Web development skills during that time and gained a level of technical savvy in my knowledge of library systems I never had before. I redesigned the library website and worked on integrating it with their electronic catalog. After a while, though, I really found myself missing the teaching that I used to do, and the contact with the patrons." Consequently, in early 2000, he took the job at the University at Buffalo Health Sciences Library and has been there ever since.

As a member of the Medical Library Association and one of its regional chapters, Brower attends annual meetings to keep in contact with colleagues and to take continuing education courses. In order to stay abreast of changing technologies, he reads the news daily and keeps a number of technology, health, and medicine newsfeeds on his personal Yahoo! page. "I've made a point of learning what I can about all kinds of educational technology, including software for building online tutorials and the like," says Brower. "Mostly, though, I'm just kind of a tech-head. I watch for new and emerging technologies all the time because I get a kick out of it."

Outside of the office, Brower does what every respectable librarian does—he collects books. His collection, however, deviates slightly from the norm because it is comprised of . . . *comic* books! Having started at age five, his collection now stands at more than seven thousand comics, dating from the mid-1940s to the present. "I'm pretty good at keeping them all preserved," he says, "but I'm lousy at organizing" (possibly one reason he is not a cataloger!). He also enjoys regular books, movies, gardening, and cycling.

Brower has a bit of advice for those interested in a career in health sciences librarianship. "First off," he says, "join the Medical Library Association." He suggests taking a health sciences library class in library school, as well as seeking a graduate assistantship in a health sciences library or a clerkship in a hospital library. "That kind of experience is pure gold."

"For those who are established librarians looking to make the switch, you might want to try volunteering some hours first, to see if it's to your liking. MLA offers a ton of continuing education workshops. Take a few and try to build up your skills in medical librarianship. Also, be sure to read up on the medical library literature so as to be current on the issues facing our field."

Brower is concerned that librarians are in an "exceptionally dangerous place right now." Now that the Internet is breaking down walls between users and information, librarians are now being perceived as "middle management" and must work to defend their value in the academic world. But if librarians hone their skills and market themselves as invaluable, the future is still a bright one.

"We thrive in the new millennium by being facilitators, instead of gatekeepers," says Brower. "We become flexible problem solvers, helping users maximize their use of information. We build new resources. We educate our users at all levels. We self-promote and we promote the library as the centerpoint of the academic community."

MICHELE R. TENNANT
Bioinformatics Librarian
Health Science Center Libraries
and UF Genetics Institute
University of Florida

Michele R. Tennant

"I had absolutely no interest in becoming a medical librarian." These could qualify as famous last words for Michele Tennant. As the bioinformatics librarian for University of Florida's (UF) Health Science Center Libraries and for the UF Genetics Institute, she is deeply involved in medical librarianship. She defends herself by saying, sheepishly, "never say never."

"Bioinformatics is the science which uses information and computer science to solve biological problems, especially those related to molecular biology and genetics," explains Tennant. In her position, which is funded by the UF Genetics Institute but housed in the Health Science Center Libraries, she serves a variety of clients. "Bioinformatics researchers tend to fall into two camps—those that build the bioinformatics tools, and those that use them to solve their biological research problems." Tennant works primarily with this second group of clients. She is the liaison librarian to genetics researchers campuswide, and is a member of the executive board of the UF Genetics Institute. Additional clients include faculty and graduate students from the college of medicine, faculty and graduate students from the departments of zoology and chemistry (at the college of liberal arts and sciences), faculty and graduate students from the Institute for Food and Agricultural Sciences, and undergraduates in genetics and related sciences. "Basically," says Tennant, "I work with any clients interested in genetics, molecular biology, and bioinformatics, from undergrad through grad/medical school, through to the faculty."

Tennant's job duties are varied. "I have two halves to my current position: one deals with traditional library services; the other half is more related to bioinformatics and genetics data retrieval and analysis." In her liaison capacity, she answers reference and basic user questions via e-mail, phone, or in person. She provides literature searches to the Genetics Institute executive board and selected departments, using citation databases such as PubMed, Current Contents Connect, Web of Science, Biological Abstracts, and BA/RRM. She participates in collection development by selecting materials dealing with molecular biology, genetics, and bioinformatics. She assists researchers in searching bioinformatics databases and also does some "data-mining" for researchers in the Genetics Institute.

Teaching occupies a significant portion of her time. Tennant provides bibliographic instruction in the use of literature databases as well as for many of the National Center for Biotechnology Information (NCBI) resources. Some of her stand-alone classes, which are offered to any faculty, student, or staff member, include "Genetics Resources for Clinicians," "NCBI Variation and Expression Resources," and "Model Organism and Molecular Protocol Resources." She is also involved with course-integrated sessions, teaching first-year college of medicine Ph.D. students, undergraduate genetics students, undergraduate biophysical chemistry students, and first-year medical students during their genetics module.

When not occupied by any of those tasks, Tennant spends time working on duties generally expected of academic librarians: committee work, publishing, presentations, and involvement in library associations. She has a number of published articles under her belt, and she is an active member of the Medical Library Association (MLA) and the Special Libraries Association (SLA). She is a frequent continuing-education instructor at annual MLA and SLA meetings, teaching courses such as "Molecular Biology and Genetics for Librarians" and "Genomics, Proteomics, and Bioinformatics for Librarians."

"I think of myself as a bridge between molecular biology/genetics and library/information science," explains Tennant. "I feel a great responsibility to help other life science and biomedical librarians learn the terminology and basic concepts in molecular biology and genetics. I also feel a great responsibility to demonstrate to biomedical researchers how valuable it can be to partner with information professionals." In that regard, she has recruited several influential biomedical researchers to speak at MLA and SLA meetings. "Obviously the librarians gain insights into the science, but the researchers learn a lot about what we are able to do for them."

In addition to staying active in professional associations, Tennant keeps up with information resources by participating in electronic discussion groups, taking continuing-education courses, and corresponding with a network of other bioinformatics librarians. She also reads library and science journals and attends genetics and bioinformatics seminars.

Librarianship was not Tennant's initial career choice. "I was sure that I was going to get my Ph.D. in biology and be a biology professor," she says. She did receive her Ph.D. in biology from Wayne State University but realized before her studies were finished that she no longer wanted to become a biology professor, nor even a laboratory biologist. At that time she was working at a University of Florida library. "I was getting a lot of encouragement from my boss at the Architecture and Fine Arts Library, who thought I would be a good librarian," she says. "He encouraged me to go to library school." Having enjoyed working in libraries in the past, and realizing that her knowledge of biology could come in handy at an academic biology library, Tennant enrolled in library school at UCLA. While there, she took every science-related library class available, taught classes in the biology department, and completed an internship with a biotechnology firm.

"It was just about that time that the [Web] was coming into being, and the very early versions of web-based tools were becoming available from NCBI," says Tennant. "It became clear to me that science librarians could move beyond the literature databases to these fact-based resources. I couldn't wait to get out of library school and start working in a science library!" She graduated with her M.L.I.S. and within six months had a position doing reference and cataloging at the medical library at University of Florida. The position evolved over the years, influenced by Tennant's skills and tenacity, to become "Bioinformatics Librarian."

What can others do to prepare for a similar career? "Take as many molecular biology and genetics classes as possible," suggests Tennant. "If possible, in library school get an internship in a bioinformatics lab, so you can learn the biology but also the culture of science. Join MLA's Molecular Biology and Genomics Special Interest Group, and SLA's Biomedical and Life Sciences Division, and you'll be part of a couple of excellent networking groups. If you already work as a librarian in an institution that has researchers in bioinformatics, but you do not necessarily work with them, make yourself visible."

Tennant, who never expected to end up where she is today, is infinitely satisfied with her career. "Being a librarian in this millennium means that we have so many options!" she says. "Do we want to provide traditional library services? Be a web designer? Work with researchers in bioinformatics? Be an informationist? All of the above? The options really are endless."

Linda Coates

LINDA COATES
Associate Director
Library Services
Zoological Society of San Diego

Linda Coates shares her library with animals. Though many librarians have made this particular claim in sarcasm, in this case it's the literal truth. "I recently had a cute young binturong visit the library," explains Coates. (A binturong is a small carnivore native to Indonesia.) "Her trainers wanted to 'socialize' her in a safe environment before she was introduced to the public. She was very well-mannered, but true to her nature she promptly leapt on one of the reading tables and by balancing on top of the upholstered chair backs, navigated from chair to chair all around the table."

Only for a zoo librarian could this type of experience be commonplace. As the associate director of Library Services at the Zoological Society of San Diego, Coates can boast about a fair share of fascinating experiences. She is responsible for selecting all information resources for the staffs of the zoo, Wild Animal Park, and Center for Reproduction of Endangered Species. Her library serves as a gateway to information for curators, veterinarians, researchers, educators, and horticulturists. "Our library's mission," she says, "is to support and collaborate with staff in collecting, organizing, preserving, and providing access to the global resources necessary to preserve and enhance our world-class zoological garden and to promote our wildlife conservation efforts."

Coates has a B.A. in zoology from the University of California at Berkeley and an M.S. in library and information science from the University of Illinois. Her first job as a professional librarian was manager of Library Services for Carle Foundation Hospital and Clinic in Urbana, Illinois. After two years, she moved on to the Biomedical Library at UCLA, becoming the Online Services coordinator for the Pacific Southwest Regional Medical Library.

"At a UCLA reception one of my good friends and I were ruminating about our dream jobs," says Coates. She told her friend that she wanted to be the librarian for the San Diego Zoo. "My dear," her friend replied, "the job doesn't exist." Her friend went on to say that the San Diego Zoo didn't even have access to OCLC, and that taking such a job would be "professional suicide."

"Two weeks after this conversation," continues Coates, "a job announcement for the 'suicidal' position was faxed to our office. I decided to abandon the *acme* of librarianship (along with earthquakes, smog, and gridlock) for beautiful Balboa Park and my dream job. The fact that there was free parking right outside the library door (in Green Gorilla parking) clinched it for me."

As the Zoological Society's first professional librarian, Coates had a lot of work ahead of her. The library had been moved many times, had changed hands often, and at one point had almost been dissolved. "My first task was convincing the volunteers assigned to keep the library doors open that we had to begin checking in the journals by their publication dates—not the dates they arrived at the zoo." For a few years Coates kept busy with retrospective conversion, computerization, thesaurus building, and indexing. At one point she was put in charge of establishing and running the society's first website. Later, Coates used her new skills to focus on the library and began building an intranet-based library information resource.

In addition to books, journals, and videos, Coates's library offers bibliographic, numeric, and textual databases to its patrons. "All materials selected for purchase must have intrinsic value to science and zoo culture and support the mission of the society," she says. "We collect everything related to exotic wildlife (husbandry, ecology, conservation, and veterinary medicine). Our horticulture collection emphasizes palms, aloes, cycads, succulents, [and] tropical and desert plants. And, of course, we have everything we can find on zoos, including history, design, and exhibitry."

"We have an extremely diverse user group ranging from Ph.D. scientists to high school students with their first job serving hamburgers at 'Koala Kitchen,'" says Coates. "We have to be able to help the educator who is trying to develop a nighttime sleep-over program as well as the vet who needs an update on malignant catarrhal fever; the bird keeper who needs a diet for a harpy eagle chick and the architect who needs to design an underwater hippo exhibit. We were actually asked how fast a hippo could charge underwater!"

"We have provided curators with information needed for our panda permit, helped our merchandising department plan an online commerce venture, and come up with the formula for rhino milk. Finding pictures for employees in our Graphics and Construction and Maintenance departments is a regular library activity. One of our greatest challenges was finding pictures of African termite mounds. A realistic model of a mound was built to contain honey and insects for orangutan enrichment."

"Our biggest challenge is space—too much and too little of it," says Coates. Too much because her users are spread over two campuses (the zoo and the Wild Animal Park) separated by sixty miles of southern California freeway. Too little space because the library is "bursting at the seams." Coates hopes that this problem will be alleviated with the building of a new library at the Wild Animal Park in 2005. To solve the problem of "too much space," Coates has made efficient use of the World Wide Web. She and her staff have built a menu-driven, low-tech Web portal to all the information resources critical to supporting the society's animal and plant collections as well as its conservation programs. The website is logically organized and free of jargon-laced terminology. Menu options include "Animals, Plants, Conservation, Reference, News, and Zoos." Hyperlinks to free resources such as government sites, academic sites, and major specialty sites are included. The Web portal also includes basic library and Web instruction, and a Zoo History Time Line.

"We've also created a number of special resources," says Coates. "One of the most important is a series of fact sheets based on key animals in our collection. The California Condor and Chacoan Peccary represent important conservation projects. Hippos, polar bears, and pygmy chimpanzees are key species in major exhibits. Each fact sheet has a standardized organization, an accompanying summary sheet, and bibliographies. The information is meticulously researched and annotated using our extensive library collection, and all fact sheets are submitted for curatorial review."

Coates finds that one of the best things about working in a zoo is that everyone has similar interests and philosophies. Zoo employees revere nature, believe in conservation and recycling, and, more important, have a great love for animals. "When a keeper asks if you would like to see his baby pictures," she says, "you can be sure you're not going to see a human baby. But then I probably have to listen to more 'Sorry, but my bird/dog/reptile ate this book' stories than other librarians."

Coates has had the privilege of hosting book signings in her library and has met many famous individuals. "I spent one marvelous afternoon listening to Roger Tory Peterson reminisce about his birding adventures while he sat in our library signing his many guidebooks. He told about a frightening accident he had while on a rafting trip. He nearly drowned and after being pulled from the water was somewhat delirious. He looked up at the top of his tent and saw hundreds of butterflies. Even though he suspected that he was hallucinating he couldn't resist trying to determine what species they were! His inquiring mind and indomitable spirit are the same characteristics I see in many of the society's employees, and this is what makes my job especially wonderful."

To maintain professional contacts and to keep up with changes in her profession, Coates belongs to the Library Special Interest Group of the American Zoo and Aquarium Association. She is also a part of the Balboa Park Library Community and recently joined the Society of California Archivists. She is active on electronic discussion groups and alerting services and monitors journals and newspapers such as the *New York Times*, *Nature*, *Science*, *Conservation Biology*, *Business Week*, and *Library Journal*. She attends workshops and conferences and is involved with the Special Libraries Association and the Medical Library Association. "My one big splurge is the International Conference of the Animal Health Information Specialists that is organized by the Veterinary Medical Librarian group affiliated with the Medical Library Association," she says. For those interested in zoo librarianship, she recommends being active in associations and monitoring general and subject-specific journals.

"Technology will obviously continue to have a tremendous impact on our lives," says Coates. "Librarians will serve increasingly as information filters and consultants, evaluating the best resources and formats and making users aware of them. Teaching information literacy will become an important part of our job because people tend to be very unsophisticated in seeking information, treating all resources as equal and not looking for the anomaly or bias. It is important that we become more proactive. By sharing our expertise we will become recognized as important to the information-seeking process." Coates hopes that, in the future, the push to free scientific information will succeed. She also hopes that something can be done for all the small, struggling museum libraries whose collections are rich and unique but, due to budget constraints, not yet part of the public record.

"Even though new electronic resources are filling our libraries, we will continue to rely heavily on paper—and lots of zoo paper is very 'gray.' It will be fascinating to observe what effects the evolutionary forces of technology, economics, and expediency have on *all* libraries," says Coates. "In the not-too-distant future, we may be looking at some completely new 'animals.'"

C. TRENTON BOYD
Veterinary Medical Librarian
Veterinary Medical Library
University of Missouri–Columbia

What is the name of a neutered male cat? What is a female beaver called? How many published articles exist regarding the treatment of hairballs in cats? Trenton Boyd knows the answers to these questions because he has had to track them down at various points during his career. "A neutered male cat is called a gib, a female beaver is a sow, and a literature search will yield only nine references to articles written about trichobezoar (hairballs)," he says. As the veterinary medical librarian at the Veterinary Medical Library of University of Missouri–Columbia, Boyd is responsible for building and maintaining a top-quality research collection on veterinary medicine. Since his library is one of only thirty-two veterinary libraries in the United States and Canada, it is safe to say that Boyd's job is both compelling and unique. It must be, for he has held this position steadfastly for thirty-three years.

C. Trenton Boyd

The Veterinary Medical Library's primary clientele are the students, staff, and faculty of the University of Missouri's College of Veterinary Medicine. "We also serve the students and faculty of the Animal Sciences Unit and the Food Science and Engineering Unit of the College of Agriculture, Food, and Natural Resources," says Boyd. "In addition, we see students from the equestrian classes at nearby Stephens College and Williams Woods College."

Since Boyd's staff consists of only two other full-time members, he handles all aspects of library work, with the exception of the cataloging and processing of books. "If I have a staff member out sick, I will be doing their job as well as my own," he explains. "If, for some reason, a scheduled student worker fails to show up to work in the evening or weekend, I must quickly either find another student worker or work the shift myself."

"I never know when I open the library in the morning what my day will entail," Boyd continues. "I have always worked under the policy that 'the patron comes first.' So, regardless of what I might be doing, that work will be put aside until I can satisfy a patron's reference question and/or literature search request." He receives reference inquiries by e-mail, fax, telephone, and walk-ins. In addition to answering reference questions, his day may be spent attending meetings, ordering books, preparing books for the bindery, receiving money for photocopies, working the circulation/reserve desk, and completing special projects such as developing lists of resources for frequently asked questions.

Boyd tends to arrive early to work in order to correspond via e-mail with his overseas colleagues before they go home for the day. This habit enables him to get a lot of work done before the day becomes busy, and also allows him to be of excellent service to his foreign colleagues. "One morning upon arriving to work I saw that I had received an ILL request via e-mail from England," he recounts. "I did not own the journal and very few places in the U.S. did, but I knew my friend in South Africa had it in his collection, so I passed the e-mail along to him. He immediately faxed the article to England. Hence, my friend in England had it on her desk when she arrived to work the next day, within twenty-four hours from when she sent the request, even though the request had been sent halfway around the world twice!"

With his extensive experience and dedication to the profession, Boyd has made significant contributions to the development of modern veterinary librarianship. "To the best of my knowledge, I have the most number of years of service in the field," he says with well-deserved pride. "I have been very blessed in my career to have been in on the ground floor of the organization of the veterinary medical library profession." Over the years, he has played an authoritative role in the growth of the specialized profession. He is one of the founding members of the Medical Library Association's (MLA) Veterinary Medical Libraries Section (VMLS) and has attended every MLA meeting since 1972. Along with two other members of VMLS, he established the International Conference of Animal Health Information Specialists. The meeting has been held three times in different European cities, and there are plans in the works for a fourth meeting to be held in Budapest, Hungary. A significant amount of interest was generated at that first international meeting. As a result, Boyd had a hand in the establishment and development of the Animal Health Information Specialists—UK and Ireland as well the European Veterinary

Librarians Group. He was invited to speak at the first Conference of the African Animal Health Information Workers, and he witnessed the development of veterinary librarian associations in Italy and France. "The three of us who planned that first meeting now look back with a great deal of pride and satisfaction at what has evolved in national and international cooperation as a result of that meeting," Boyd says.

Boyd's interest in library science was influenced, oddly enough, by his lifelong fascination with genealogy. While studying for his undergraduate degree in agriculture (with a major in wildlife conservation), he spent a great deal of free time pursuing his genealogy at the State Historical Society of Missouri. "I soon knew everyone in the society, and it was almost as if I worked there," he says. "One day, in conversation, one of the reference librarians suggested I might consider a career in library science as she thought I was such an adept researcher. I pursued her idea by going to the library school and talking to one of the student advisors. He assured me that with a science background, I would be in high demand, and that generally science librarians earned more money than other types of librarians." Boyd decided to take a course to see what library school was like but was hesitant to consult with his advisor in wildlife conservation about his plans. "He was a renowned researcher and had spent many years in the field. I was absolutely convinced he would not understand my desire to take a library school course. However, much to my surprise, he was very enthusiastic and supportive of the idea. He said as a researcher he spent hours and hours in the outdoors, but there was a need for people on the inside to be able to understand and preserve the data collected. Well, you could have knocked me over with a feather, but the rest is history!"

After graduating with his M.A. in library science from the University of Missouri, Boyd's first job as a professional librarian was science librarian at Wichita State University in Wichita, Kansas. After two years there, he learned of an opening at the University of Missouri for a veterinary medical librarian. He applied and got the job. "I was the first professional librarian at the Veterinary Medical Library and I am still here thirty-three years later!" he says.

According to Boyd, veterinary librarianship is unique in a number of ways. Not only are there so few veterinary libraries in comparison with other types of libraries, the discipline relies heavily on what is called "gray literature," or information that is difficult to locate. Tracking down this type of literature for purchase is one of Boyd's greatest challenges. "There are only a handful of mainstream publishers for veterinary medicine," he explains. "All of the other books are published by small presses, associations, or by the author. Many publications have a very limited press run, so you hope to get your order placed in time. Over the years I have become pretty successful at doing this. My reward comes when another library is seeking an item for which I am the only holding library in OCLC."

Another unique aspect of the profession is the fact that a veterinarian is responsible for the health of all animals except man. Hence, veterinary librarians are responsible for access to information regarding all these organisms. "Within the last fifteen years, the development of alternative farm animals and the American penchant for exotic pets have turned the whole world of the veterinarian, and in turn the veterinary librarian, upside down," says Boyd. "Almost overnight, librarians were bombarded with requests for care and treatment of llamas, alpacas, ostriches, and rheas. Initially, the literature was scanty at best and much of the initial knowledge available came from the breeders themselves. Then came the wave of questions for pocket pets such as the African hedgehog and the sugar glider. The librarians stayed busy on VETLIB-L, the electronic discussion group for veterinary librarians, exchanging useful sources of information until the first books were published on each subject."

Boyd spends many frustrating moments trying to inform faculty and students that not all the answers they are seeking can be found on the Internet. "Veterinary journals have been very slow to come up online," he says. This, combined with the "gray literature" factor, forces Boyd and other veterinary librarians to constantly educate library users regarding the limits of the Internet for veterinary information.

"I can cite several subjects in which the most important research was performed in the years prior to online databases," Boyd says. "For instance, the best studies and still the best information on poisonous plants can be found in the literature of the 1920s and 1930s. I tell students this when they fail to find current information on a topic, but they are still reluctant to search the manual indices."

Aside from these frustrations, Boyd's job comes with its fair share of excitement. "Without a doubt the biggest and most time-consuming project I was involved in was one that I was told in library school that very few librarians would ever have the opportunity to do—the planning of a new library!" When the College of Veterinary Medicine expanded its facilities, Boyd was given free reign to plan the utilization of the library's allotted 6,725 square feet of space. The huge project, which finally involved moving 22,000 volumes to the new facility, was a welcome challenge for Boyd.

Another project special to Boyd involved the Miss America Pageant. The woman crowned Miss America for 1990, Debbye Turner, was a third-year student from the College of Veterinary Medicine at the University of Missouri. Consequently, it fell to Boyd to collect any and all information, in print or otherwise, regarding the pageant, the winner, and all related news articles. "The quest began as I visited the newsstands every week to see if any magazines had articles about her," says Boyd. "I called in favors from every librarian I had ever helped in my career, asking them to send me stories from their local newspapers if Debbye made an appearance in their city. I videotaped all of her national appearances. It turned out that Debbye was the most requested speaker and most popular Miss America in the history of the organization. She changed cities, on average, every two days. She made more than two hundred personal appearances across the nation during her tenure, so you can see how difficult it was to try to collect everything written about her. I did manage to gather enough information about her to fill three large boxes. Unfortunately, it is still waiting to be properly organized."

Boyd is a member of a number of professional associations. "There is truly nothing that can compare to meeting people one-on-one," he says. "Friendships develop that allow you to ask for help in ways that you would never have been able to do before. As a result, the quality of service you can offer your clientele improves considerably." He is a member of MLA, its Midcontinental Chapter, and three of its subsections: VMLS, History of the Health Sciences Section, and the International Cooperation Section. He has achieved the notable status of being a distinguished member of MLA's AHIP (Academy of Health Information Professionals). He is also a member of the European Association for Health Information and Libraries (EAHIL) and its subsection, European Veterinary Libraries Group. In addition, he is active in the Animal Health Information Specialists—UK and Ireland, the World Association for the History of Veterinary Medicine, and the American Veterinary History Society.

His background in wildlife conservation has helped Boyd considerably in his work. "I like to tell people that, as an undergraduate, I took almost every 'ology' class that was offered, including zoology, ichthyology, ecology, mammology, ornithology, and dendrology. The only one I missed was herpetology. Consequently, I had a very good grounding in taxonomy and medical terms."

For those interested in pursuing a career in veterinary librarianship, Boyd says, "Try to familiarize yourself with the profession as much as possible. Monitor VETLIB-L, the electronic discussion group for veterinary librarians. If possible, attend the Medical Library Association annual meeting, and in particular the VMLS business meeting. This will give you an opportunity to meet many of the veterinary medical librarians. The group is very friendly and will be happy to answer any questions you may have. Also, if possible, visit a veterinary library."

"The job market is very tight for our specialty," he continues. "There are a limited number of positions, and most of the present veterinary librarians have made the job their life's work, so no vacancies occur unless a retirement takes place. Personally, I think a future trend will be the hiring of veterinarians as librarians. There have already been several instances of recent graduates from veterinary school who have then pursued a library degree. Unfortunately, they found there were no openings in veterinary libraries and went on to pursue other things." Boyd does mention, however, that in the near future a significant percentage of the current veterinary medical librarians will retire, which will leave those positions open for new librarians.

Boyd has a number of activities lined up for his own future retirement. He is an avid collector of postcards about Missouri, veterinary medicine, and rock 'n' roll. "To the best of my knowledge, I have the largest collection in existence for each subject category. The Missouri collection has frequently been used by authors seeking illustrations for their books and by historic preservationists trying to document how buildings used to look. My long-term goal is to do some desktop publishing using my collection as basis for publishing illustrative books about Missouri." Boyd is also looking forward to spending more time pursuing his genealogical research. Since genealogy is what led him to librarianship in a roundabout way, one might say that he has come full circle.

LINDA ANN KACZMARCZYK
Clinical Librarian for Pediatrics
Connecticut Children's Medical Center
Hartford Hospital

Linda Kaczmarczyk uses information to help provide quality patient care to sick children. In her role as clinical librarian for the Department of Pediatrics at Connecticut Children's Medical Center, she finds a great deal of satisfaction

Linda Ann Kaczmarczyk

knowing that, on any given day, her work might help to make a child's stay in the hospital easier or that an article she found will help a physician make a critical healthcare decision. "In my role I am responsible for the access and rapid delivery of medical information using a variety of media in support of patient care, education, and research," she says. "Whenever I'm told that the information I provide helps in some way, it just makes my day."

Clinical librarianship is unique in many ways. "While most medical librarians operate within the library," Kaczmarczyk explains, "clinical librarians actually go out to patient care areas accompanying the healthcare team as they conduct their clinical rounds, or [they] can be found in attendance at conferences and meetings." She says that by being an active participant, the clinical librarian is immediately accessible to any member of the healthcare team (physicians, nurses, medical students, clinical pharmacists, clinical dieticians, therapists, social workers, etc.), and questions can be posed directly when they arise. Knowing the patient's history and being present for any concerns raised during rounds affords the librarian a unique perspective in answering specific questions. "The clinical librarian has a better grasp as to why a particular question may have been asked, what other factors are involved in the care of the patient, and what information is already known."

"With this background information, quality-filtered, case-specific articles can be returned to the team along with a search within hours," Kaczmarczyk continues. "Sometimes just knowing a little more about the patient helps in selecting appropriate articles. Hearing something in the history may make a difference as to why a certain article may be included. The articles provided can then aid in clinical decision making for that particular patient."

In addition to case-specific articles, the clinical librarian provides information for conferences, presentations, publications, and research. Any person involved with health care might turn to the librarian for critical information. "Once the skills, knowledge, accuracy, and speed of the clinical librarian are recognized, they become a valuable, respected, and trusted member of the healthcare team."

Kaczmarczyk's major responsibility is performing literature searches in support of patient care. She also staffs the circulation/reference desk and teaches classes on information retrieval. She attends rounds, conferences, meetings, and participates in collection development. Her primary clientele are the healthcare professionals working in the hospital as well as the outside attending physicians. "These can range from medical students, residents, physicians, and specialists within the hospital such as gastroenterologists, nephrologists, and neonatologists to nurses, pharmacists, dieticians, social workers, physical therapists, or even consumers," she says. "My questions can range from a resident who needs to present at a case management conference to an attending specialist who has just seen a patient, or a pharmacist who needs the dosing of a particular drug for a child."

A typical day for Kaczmarczyk begins by picking up voice mail and reading e-mail. She then works on questions or searches until it is time to go on rounds. The length of time she spends on rounds can vary, as can the number of questions that arise and from whom. "Some days a nurse might need some information on a particular disease, or the attending physician may ask if there is anything in the literature about efficacy of a particular treatment, or a certain journal article may be requested."

"There are days when I can tell that there is a question that someone needs answered but hasn't asked," says Kaczmarczyk. "These are perceived questions and when an article or two are returned to the person, he or she is very grateful. Sometimes I might go up to a person after rounds and ask if they need or want any information about something that was discussed."

When she returns to her office in the medical library, Kaczmarczyk begins searching databases such as Medline to locate answers to questions that arose during rounds. She then reads the articles and filters them for quality and sends copies of the most relevant ones to the requestor, along with the search and any notes she might have made. Her turnaround time for a search and articles is usually the same day or within twenty-four hours. "There are times when I think that I have a handle on my tasks for the day," she says, "but then a person calls with a search request that needs to be done immediately. Because this involves patient care, it must get done before leaving for the day. Some days can be a little hectic or longer than usual, but this is what makes my job exciting and challenging."

Kaczmarczyk has a B.A. in biology from the College of Our Lady of the Elms in Chicopee, Massachusetts, and she is certified as a medical technologist. For a number of years she worked in the Division of Microbiology at Hartford Hospital. "Clinical librarianship came about as a career change for me," she says. "One day at the end of a management class at the hospital, I began talking with one of the medical librarians about what she did. I had always been interested in librarianship as far back as high school, but I liked science and didn't realize the two could be meshed." With the encouragement of two librarians, she took classes part-time and received her M.L.S. from Southern Connecticut State University. After graduating, she held various positions and soon realized that she really enjoyed clinical librarianship. "I was able to return to Hartford Hospital in a position that was entirely clinical and worked under Gertrude Lamb, founder of the first clinical librarian program at the University of Missouri at Kansas City School of Medicine." Later on, the Connecticut Children's Medical Center (CCMC) was formed. Since the medical library at Hartford Hospital provides services to CCMC, Kaczmarczyk was able to continue acting as the clinical librarian for the Department of Pediatrics.

"What I find challenging and exciting is that every day brings something new and I still get excited about what I do," says Kaczmarczyk. "I'm constantly learning and gaining knowledge whenever I work on a search question. There is always the element of surprise because I never know what kind of day it will be. Will there be many questions? Will they be easy or difficult to answer? How soon does the person need the answer? Who will be asking? Have I done something like this before?"

"You learn to prioritize and to expect the unexpected, but that's what makes it fun. You never know how the information provided may have made a difference in that precise moment for someone." On one particular day, Kaczmarczyk was on rounds with an attending physician and several residents, who were examining a patient. After a few minutes, the attending physician looked up at her and asked if she could find out if there was any correlation between the condition the patient had and a recent procedure. He then said, "It's so nice having a librarian on rounds." This type of comment is what keeps Kaczmarczyk excited about her job.

She says, "If you like working in a medical setting and have a strong service orientation, hold what you learn in confidence, like being a team player, can deal with pressure, and enjoy finding specific answers and always learning something new, clinical librarianship is one of the best ways to affect patient care. Sometimes there is a feeling of discouragement, but the feeling of satisfaction in having helped someone always makes me smile."

Kaczmarczyk keeps up with technology and the profession of librarianship by taking continuing-education classes, reading professional journals, and attending professional conferences. She is a member of the

Medical Library Association (MLA) and has certification at the senior level in MLA's Academy of Health Information Professionals. She is also a member of the Special Libraries Association as well as regional and state associations such as Connecticut Association of Health Sciences Librarians and North Atlantic Health Sciences Libraries.

"Being a librarian in the new millennium means keeping up with technology but not completely discarding or ignoring what is older," says Kaczmarczyk. "The Internet is wonderful and has made life so much easier, but sometimes it is a book that has the answer. We need to be advocates and teachers for what is new and upcoming, but we also must remember to keep a human connection with people that we help."

MARY WHISNER
Assistant Librarian for Reference Services
Gallagher Law Library
University of Washington School of Law

With a bachelor's degree in philosophy and a law degree from Harvard, one might wonder how Mary Whisner came to be a librarian at an academic law library. The story is similar to that of many law librarians, who commonly come into the field after having tried other things for a while.

Mary Whisner

Whisner received her undergraduate degree from the University of Washington. After graduation, and while working as a secretary in the philosophy department, she began considering different career paths. "Somebody advised me that the market for librarians was so bad I should not try to go to library school," she says. "Others said that law school was interesting. It seemed worth a try." Whisner was admitted to Harvard Law School and enjoyed her time there. "Law librarianship was not a career goal then, but I remember being impressed by the law librarian who gave lectures to the first-year students on legal research and telling my friends that he had both a law degree and a library degree."

In the three years after law school, Whisner had three legal jobs: as a law clerk to a federal judge, as a staff attorney for the National Labor Relations Board, and as an attorney with a civil rights group. The last job, funded by a fellowship program, gave her the opportunity to participate in classes and activities at Georgetown's law school. "I found that I enjoyed the academic activities more than litigation," she says. "As I was exploring what to do after my fellowship ended, a couple of people encouraged me to talk to law librarians." She contacted the director of the law library at Loyola University in New Orleans and was hired on a temporary basis to help move the library to a new building. After the move, she stayed on for a while to update library guides and work in reference.

"This job gave me a wonderful introduction to librarianship and confirmed my decision to change careers," says Whisner. "I entered library school at Louisiana State University, where I got my M.L.I.S. I worked part-time in the law library at LSU while I was in library school and gained valuable experience."

At an annual meeting of the American Association of Law Libraries (AALL), Whisner interviewed for jobs and was hired as a reference librarian at the Gallagher Law Library of the University of Washington. She has been there ever since. She began as reference librarian, then added some middle management responsibilities and became head of reference, and is now assistant librarian for Reference Services.

Whisner manages the reference department and provides front-line reference services to library patrons. She also supervises the law librarianship students who work in reference, represents the department in library-wide committees, and gives guest lectures on research topics. "I have a wonderful job," she says. During a typical day she begins by checking e-mail, a task she often finds difficult to keep up with. Most days, whether in the morning, afternoon, or evening, she has a shift in the Reference Office where she helps library patrons locate the legal information they need. If she has a few moments to herself, she works on projects, such as updating Reference Office documentation, or reads professional literature. She often has meetings such as collection development, reference, library council, and law school committee meetings. Several times each quarter Whisner delivers guest lectures to classes regarding research and must spend time preparing the presentations as well as the handouts. In the spare time she has after her long list of duties, Whisner works on writing projects. She writes articles for the law library column in the school newspaper, has a column on reference for *Law Library Journal*, and helps to publish a manual for legal researchers in the state.

"My biggest challenges involve keeping up with the little things," Whisner admits. "I get snowed under by my e-mail. Meanwhile, my physical in-box fills up too frequently with publishers' ads, professional reading, and miscellaneous publications—and then they are stacked up on my desktop, unsorted and unread. Putting together the biweekly reference schedule requires concentration because there are a lot of details to keep track of. While I enjoy the variety of my job, sometimes I do find that I have too many balls in the air."

In her day-to-day work, Whisner deals with a variety of library patrons. "Our primary patrons are the students, faculty, and staff of the University of Washington School of Law," she explains. "However, the library is open to the public and is heavily used by a wide variety of people—members of the public, attorneys, and undergraduate students, graduate students, and faculty from the rest of the university." Whisner enjoys working with the law students and professors, who are bright, verbal, and well educated. "Some are more technically sophisticated than others, some are better organized than others, and some have better interpersonal skills than others," she says. "Happily, though, they tend to be quite good-natured."

Members of the public come to the law library because of legal issues affecting their lives, such as landlord-tenant problems, child custody disputes, or employment discrimination. "It is important that they have access to legal information, and I am very glad that our library is open to them," Whisner says. "Working with them presents different challenges (and rewards) than working with our elite students and faculty."

Whisner belongs to a number of professional associations, including AALL, Law Librarians of Puget Sound, WestPac (the Western Pacific Chapter of AALL), the American Library Association, and the Washington State Bar Association. She attends conferences and association meetings when possible, attends continuing legal education programs, and goes to training offered by vendors such as LexisNexis and Westlaw. She keeps up with technology by trying out new databases, taking classes, and visiting exhibits and demonstrations at convention halls. She has found that using her newly acquired personal digital assistant, which she calls her "gizmo," has been a good exercise in keeping up with innovative technology.

"I'd like to encourage other librarians to think about academic law librarianship," says Whisner. "Our library has benefited from librarians coming here from other types of libraries. In recent years, we have hired librarians whose experience was in public libraries, in academic libraries, in law firm libraries, and in special libraries." She explains that the job market for academic law librarians is national, and most libraries advertise positions at both the local and national levels. "There are about 180 American Bar Association–accredited law schools in the United States, each with a law library. The more widely you can apply, the more opportunities you will have." Whisner goes on to explain that although a J.D. is not always required for a job in academic law librarianship, some libraries prefer a law degree for reference and public services positions. Librarians without law degrees will have more opportunities in technical services.

When asked what it means to be a librarian in this new millennium, Whisner responds, "I do not think the changing of the calendar changed the meaning of our profession very much. We are still professionals who help people find and use information—whether it is in books lined up on a shelf or on computers linked in a World Wide Web."

It does not appear that law librarianship as a profession will disappear anytime soon. "Law is a field that looks to the past, so law libraries—especially academic law libraries—must maintain, preserve, and provide access to cases and statutes from years and centuries past," says Whisner. The same can be said for the cases and statutes of the future. For as long as legal documentation continues to be produced, there will be a need for law librarians.

Cindy L. Chick

CINDY L. CHICK
Information Resources Systems Coordinator
Latham & Watkins

"I think a law librarian in a firm setting is a hero on an almost daily basis," says Cindy Chick. "Sometimes it's just the little things you do, or sometimes it's the really exceptional research that you produce. Either way, the attorneys are under pressure, and contrary to the popular stereotype, they're very appreciative of the help you give them. You really become an integral part of the team. That's very satisfying, and a little addicting."

As the information resources systems coordinator at Latham & Watkins law firm, Chick is an "integral part" of the library, records, and docket departments. One of her primary duties is to expand, update, and maintain the collection of links and other library content on the firm's

Intranet. She also works on the development of databases and other technology projects as needed by different departments. "To a great extent, it's very much a 'project management' type of job," she explains. "The technology team handles the actual programming that's required. My job is to talk to the different departments to see what their needs are, then define projects to meet those needs and work with the technology team to explain the requirements of the projects."

Chick knew that she wanted to be a librarian at a very early stage in life. "I think it all started when I was eight, when I designed a card checkout system for my books," she says. She received her master's degree in library and information science, with a specialization in law librarianship, from UCLA.

"I had worked in college libraries while working on my B.A. in English from California State University, but I really didn't know anything about special libraries. The UCLA graduate school had a two-year program and the second year you had to pick a specialization. After attending a career day at which several special librarians spoke, including Marie Wallace, a law librarian, I decided to give law a try." While in library school, Chick gained valuable experience by working in a variety of law libraries, including the Western Center of Law and Poverty, the L.A. County Law Library, and a Century City law firm library.

"I've been working in law firms ever since," says Chick. "Somehow I had a knack (notice the use of the past tense) for choosing what would ultimately prove to be a string of unsuccessful law firms for which to work. Almost every firm on my resume is no longer in business. Though I stayed at some firms for up to eight years, I was actually forced to move around a bit. It may not have seemed like a good thing at the time, but it probably worked to my benefit in terms of career development."

For most of her career, Chick has been a solo librarian. "This meant I had to be a jack-of-all-trades," she says. Despite a certain amount of clerical work, Chick enjoyed her jobs and was particularly fond of analyzing procedures and looking for ways to make her department more efficient. "When computers became powerful enough to have a real impact in my environment, I was hooked. I started taking computer classes, often on database-related topics, and learned skills that I quickly found invaluable."

Chick finds her current job to be completely different from her previous ones. "This job was a big change for me," she says. "I was used to doing research, managing a department, supervising staff, and just generally having work thrown at me constantly during the course of a day. On any given day I never knew if I'd have enough time to make any progress on my projects and, of course, could be interrupted constantly. Now, though there are always interruptions, I can actually have several hours at a stretch to just concentrate on something. What a concept!"

The primary clientele of the Information Resources department include the attorneys, paralegals, and staff of the firm, and, ultimately, the clients of the firm. However, Chick works more directly with librarians, records managers, and docket staff who are, in turn, trying to meet the demands of the lawyers and staff. "It's an interesting change, going from being a solo librarian to working closely with a fairly large group of professionals in many different offices," she says. "There's great synergy that results from working closely with others in your field, and I'm very much enjoying it, especially after years of being solo."

Chick's routine varies from day to day. In the mornings, she begins by checking e-mail to see if there are any technical problems that need to be addressed right away. When those issues are taken care of, she often has meetings to attend. "Lots of them," she adds. "After all, my job requires listening to the needs of my clientele, learning about problems they need to solve, and identifying the requirements of any technology projects that might help them."

Chick is heavily involved with training. "Right now we have an Intranet application that we're introducing to the paralegals and attorneys," she explains, "so I'm spending quite a bit of time trying to get everyone up and running with the system and making presentations to show people what the application can do." She also organizes virtual training sessions, using conferencing software to conduct training on a variety of topics for employees across firm offices globally.

"Some days I think we should add 'nagging' to my job description," she says. "I'm an equal opportunity nagger. I nag everybody. If I fail to adequately nag someone, I usually pay for it in the end. It's not the most pleasant part of the job, but unfortunately in this position, it's absolutely necessary in order to get things done. I need to keep checking with technology on the status of our various projects, nag our vendors to make sure they're doing what's needed, nag the librarians to make sure they've given me the information I need, etc. Of course, being pleasant while nagging is critical, and really quite the art form."

Chick says that encouraging and initiating change is the most challenging part of her job. "I can come up with the best application in the world, but if the librarians, records managers, et cetera, don't see the value in it, all that hard work will go to waste and we can't move forward. It's essential that I do my job in terms of interpreting what they need. Then I try very hard to make my applications so useful and so easy to use, that no one can resist!"

Ever on the lookout for technology news, Chick reads both library-related journals and technology journals such as *PC World* and *PC Magazine*. "It's very important to have an idea what's going on in the 'outside world,'" she says. "At every level from simple to sophisticated, you can find applications that can help us do our jobs better, but do not have libraries as their primary audience. Since we don't often have the funds to develop applications from scratch, we need to keep a close eye on technology developed for other purposes to see if they can be tweaked to meet our needs." Chick is a member of the American Association of Law Libraries, the Special Libraries Association, and the Southern California Association of Law Libraries. She attends professional seminars and conferences and takes UCLA extension courses related to technology.

For those interested in librarianship careers within law firms, Chick says that the job market is fairly stable. "There's not a lot of movement in the higher-level positions, but there is a need for staff in entry-level positions." She feels that this is bound to change soon, since there are likely to be large numbers of law librarians retiring in the near future. "My expectation would be that the job market will be very good in the coming years, and the people going into the entry-level jobs now will be well-positioned in the future."

Chick also says that in law firm settings, the majority of librarians do not have law degrees. A law degree is not expected or required. There is a certain amount of pressure, however, involved with working in a law firm. "You definitely have to justify your existence on an ongoing basis," she says. Chick feels that this is true within the world of general librarianship as well. "We each have the challenge of proving our worth as librarians, with our overall view of information and organization," she says. "If we can't do that, then librarianship will eventually cease to exist as a profession." This seems a heavy burden to bear, but like many others in the field, Chick finds this pressure motivating.

In addition to her regular job, Cindy Chick is the co-editor and publisher of *LLRX*, a web newsletter on law-related research and technology issues. For more information, go to http://www.llrx.com.

SAMPLE JOB DESCRIPTIONS

Academic Medical Librarians

Environment

Academic medical librarians, also known as academic health sciences librarians, most often work in medical school libraries. Depending upon the size and organization of the library, they may be assigned certain public services duties (such as reference, teaching, or circulation) or certain technical services duties (such as cataloging, acquisitions, collection management, web management, or systems management). In very small libraries, they may be expected to be proficient in a number of these areas. Academic medical librarians generally serve students, faculty, physicians, nurses, general healthcare consumers, and numerous other patron groups.

Responsibilities

Locate print and electronic health-related resources for patrons

Instruct end users in the retrieval and application of health information

Develop content and design materials for instructional purposes

Evaluate advanced information technologies as related to medicine

Develop, design, navigate, and maintain websites

Select and purchase books, journals, and other health-related resources

Organize books, journals, and other resources for ease of use

Work with faculty to integrate library and searching skills into the curriculum

Share resources with other libraries through interlibrary loan

Plan, budget, and manage library programs and services

Work on teams and serve on committees within the library and the organization

Engage in research, publishing, and other scholarly activities

Education and Training

A master's degree in library and information science from an ALA-accredited institution is required. Prior experience in the basic or applied sciences, health care, or computer technology is recommended but not required.

Recommended Memberships

Medical Library Association (MLA) and associated regional chapters

Local medical library associations

Hospital/Clinical Librarians

Environment

Clinical librarians most often work in hospital settings. Many work in one-person libraries and are therefore responsible for a variety of duties, including administrative work. In larger hospital libraries, duties are distributed among various staff members. Clinical librarians work closely with physicians, nurses, allied health professionals, therapists, patients, and administrators.

Responsibilities

Locate print and electronic health-related resources for hospital personnel and patients

Evaluate advanced information technologies as related to medicine

Develop, design, navigate, and maintain websites

Select and purchase books, journals, and other health-related resources

Organize books, journals, and other resources for ease of use

Plan, budget, and manage library programs and services

Work on teams and collaborate on projects with other hospital personnel

Instruct end users in the retrieval and application of health information

Education and Training

A master's degree in library and information science from an ALA-accredited institution is required. Prior experience in the basic or applied sciences, health care, or computer technology is recommended but not required.

Recommended Memberships

Medical Library Association (MLA) and associated regional chapters

Hospital Libraries Section (HLS) of MLA

Local medical library associations

Academic Law Librarians

Environment

Academic law librarians generally work in law school libraries. Duties vary according to staff size; some law librarians are solely responsible for reference duties, some are responsible for technical services duties, and others are involved in both areas. They primarily offer services to law school students and faculty.

Responsibilities

Locate print and electronic legal information for patrons

Instruct end users in the retrieval and application of legal information

Develop content and design materials for instructional purposes

Evaluate advanced information technologies that are related to law

Develop, design, navigate, and maintain websites

Select and purchase books, journals, and other law-related information

Organize books, journals, and other resources for ease of use

Work with faculty to integrate library and searching skills into the curriculum

Share resources with other libraries through interlibrary loan

Plan, budget, and manage library programs and services

Work on teams and serve on committees within the library and the organization

Engage in research, publishing, and other scholarly activities

Education and Training

A master's degree in library and information science from an ALA-accredited institution is required. A Juris Doctorate (law degree) is generally required for reference positions as well as library directorship positions. A J.D. is not usually required for technical services positions. Some previous experience in the field of law (as a legal aid, for example) is recommended but not required.

Recommended Memberships

American Association of Law Libraries (AALL)

Special Libraries Association (SLA)

Regional and local law library associations

Corporate Law Librarians

Environment

Corporate law librarians work in law firms or private corporations. They may work as the solo librarian or as part of a larger library team. Their primary patrons, generally, are the firm's attorneys or other firm employees.

Responsibilities

Locate print and electronic legal information for attorneys or other patrons

Perform various levels of research for attorneys

Instruct firm employees in the retrieval of legal information, particularly using electronic databases

Evaluate advanced information technologies as related to the field of law

Develop, design, navigate, and maintain websites

Select and purchase books, journals, and other law-related resources

Organize books, journals, and other resources for ease of use

Plan, budget, and manage library programs and services

Work on teams and collaborate on projects with other firm personnel

Education and Training

A master's degree in library and information science from an ALA-accredited institution is required. A Juris Doctorate (law degree) is not usually required. Previous experience in a legal setting (legal aide, for example) is recommended but not required.

Recommended Memberships

American Association of Law Libraries (AALL)

Special Libraries Association (SLA)

Regional and local law library associations

Notes

1. Robert M. Braude, "On the Origin of a Species: Evolution of Health Sciences Librarianship," *Bulletin of the Medical Library Association* 85, no. 1 (1997): 1–10.

2. Robert M. Braude, "History of Health Sciences Librarianship," from *Health Sciences Environment and Librarianship in Health Sciences Libraries* (Chicago: Medical Library Association, 1999): 139–80.

3. Carla J. Funk, "What's Special about Special Libraries? The Practice Environment of the Health Sciences Librarian," *INSPEL* 32, no. 4 (1998): 205–11.

4. Michael J. Schau, "Law Librarianship: A Unique Vocation," *Journal of Educational Media and Library Sciences* 39, no. 2 (2001): 106–13.

5. Education for a Career in Law Librarianship: Frequently Asked Questions, 2002, available at http://www.aallnet.org/committee/tfedu/education.html. Accessed 22 August 2002.

CHAPTER 6

Library
Directorship

Becoming the director of a library is not an automatic career goal for most librarians. The majority of those in the field of library and information science advance steadily throughout their careers without even considering an administrative or upper-level management position. This is the correct choice for many people, since library directorship is not a job for everyone. There are those individuals, however, who seem to be cut from a unique mold, one perfectly suited to positions of leadership. These are the people who, whether consciously or by fate, move through their careers with the ultimate goal of directorship in mind. When it comes to library directorship, the old adage "you either have it or you don't" rings true.

A library director has overall authority and responsibility for the planning, direction, and operation of a library or a group of libraries. Regardless of the type of library involved—public, academic, school, and so on—the director plays a key role in shaping the library and determining its function within the institution or the community. The director establishes the library's mission and goals and works to ensure that all library activities support those goals. He or she oversees all planning processes, manages the budget, authorizes expenditures, and supervises financial planning and fund-raising efforts. The director provides leadership and direction to the library staff and guides the recruitment, selection, and evaluation of library employees. Above all, the director is the most visible and vocal representative of the library as a whole and must strive to represent and protect the library's interests within the institution as well as to outside organizations.

To be successful at any or all of those responsibilities requires certain skills and personality attributes. At a minimum, it is important for a library director to have good communication skills, consensus-building skills, leadership skills, political skills, intuition, and networking skills. He or she "must be empathetic, a decent human being, nurturing, even-tempered, and an advocate, and able to synthesize and represent the ideas of others."[1] Moreover, a director should be a go-getter and a visionary, capable of gauging the direction in which technology and society are headed and using those facts to secure the library's position in years to come.

Experience is key to success as a library director. Most positions require a minimum of five to ten years of experience in progressively administrative library jobs. A director should have a rich background of knowledge and experience in order to be able to deal effectively with the demands of the job. Though the master's degree is sufficient for most director positions, some institutions such as colleges or universities require an additional master's degree or even a doctorate.[2] In most cases, however, it is not an impressive educational background that defines a successful library leader but rather a solid combination of experience and personal attributes.

As the majority of current library directors reach retirement age in the near future, there will be many opportunities for librarians in the workforce to move into administrative positions. Soon the library world will be calling for experienced librarians to take on these vital roles of leadership and to help shape the future of librarianship. Who is ready for the challenge?

SPOTLIGHTS

Sheila Ross Henderson

SHEILA ROSS HENDERSON
Library Director
Pasadena Public Library System
Pasadena, Tex.

There are some to whom leadership comes naturally. This seems to be the case for Sheila Henderson, who has served as an upper-level administrator in four libraries throughout her career. Though she claims that becoming a library director was "happenstance" rather than a career choice, her achievements and overall success prove that she has found her niche in the field of librarianship. For Henderson, library directorship is a perfect fit.

Henderson has been director of the Pasadena Public Library for more than three years. Looking back, she classifies her role in the beginning as being very ubiquitous. When she was appointed to the position, the library had been without a director for more than a year. "My first responsibility was to troubleshoot, mediate, define, set parameters, and decipher and interpret just about everything in an effort to pull the team together. A vision had to be articulated, mission redefined, goals established, objectives agreed upon, and a strategy for implementation put in place. More important, staff needed to feel valued and have their jobs redefined in tandem with the technological environment that had been established." Henderson has never been one to shirk her duties or to avoid difficult situations. In fact, she claims to have little patience with people who want a free ride or who are unwilling to pull their own weight. So, daunting as her list of initial responsibilities may have seemed, Henderson jumped right into the fray and got to work.

Was she successful? Well, under her leadership, the Pasadena Public Library has won six awards and four grants in a little over two years. The library's programs and services have been brought into the public eye through positive media attention. Henderson herself won Library Director of the Year for 2002, an honor awarded by the Texas Municipal Library Directors Association (TMLDA). Success may be a relative term, but in this case it's fairly obvious that Henderson met, and even exceeded, the challenging goals she set for herself at the onset.

"I am happy to say that I have gone from being the 'hands-on director' to the 'that-a-boy' coach," says Henderson. "It is a great feeling to know that managers and supervisors are equipped to solve problems and make appropriate decisions." Now that the library is on its toes again, her primary duty is to oversee the Central and Branch libraries and to offer guidance to a staff of seventeen professionals and forty-four paraprofessionals.

"It is my practice to articulate regularly my vision for the library, meet as needed with managers to develop a conceptual framework from which to operate, and provide essential tools in the form of information, equipment, resource persons, and seminars and workshops," says Henderson. "My workday can be described as anything but routine. I use my planner only as a guide to what may—sometimes should—occur during the day."

"I am a proponent of using technology to make my life easier," she continues. "Consequently, I use voice-mail to communicate not only with my staff but with myself as well. Oftentimes during the night I will call the office and leave messages for myself and other staff. Sometimes it is just an idea that is tooling around in my head and I need to get it out so that I may sleep. Other times, it is the 'big one' that may lead to a major project. The big ones have netted us awards and recognition for which I am very pleased."

Henderson is never short on these big ideas. "I have a reputation that suggests when I say 'I have an idea,' it is best to run for cover or take a long vacation," she admits. "For example, we won the grand prize award for promoting A&E Network's *Great Gatsby* television movie. It started fairly small and grew until the entire community had an opportunity to participate." Another program stemming from one of Henderson's big ideas was the library's Reading Rodeo contest held in conjunction with the annual Pasadena Rodeo. Designed to attract teens to the library, the Reading Rodeo awarded a computer and other items to teenagers who had written the best book reviews. "The teens that participated will be invited to serve on a teen advisory committee to help plan the new teen services area that will be constructed as part of a renovation project. It was not planned that these teens would be drafted to assist us; the idea came to me the day of the presentations. The participants were enthusiastic and seemed quite industrious. I simply saw an opportunity to tap into their energy and peer knowledge."

"The most life-changing event held at our library by far has been the World Trade Center exhibit," says Henderson. The exhibit, assembled by two retired Port Authority officers from New Jersey and New York, had been shown in forty-six locations throughout the United States before making its way to Pasadena. "We were the first library to host the display. In the nineteen hours of viewing time, over 1,100 people passed through the exhibit hall. Very few people exited without showing emotion; many people were in tears."

Despite many such innovative projects and programs, Henderson finds that her most difficult task is raising the profile of the library and establishing the net value of library service in the eyes of the community. "I believe we have been very creative in our approach to promoting our programs and publicizing what we do," she says. "We have developed an impressive database of contacts through our various attempts to increase awareness of the library's needs and to promote special services. Each project we have undertaken has consumed a vast amount of energy and personal time and very few resources. That takes creativity and ingenuity. Yet, we too often continue to get blank stares when talking about services offered at the library and virtually no response to requests for donations or upon inviting individuals and businesses to join the Friends organization. We continue to search for the key that will unlock the door to the fund-raising dilemma."

"My staff is famous for pulling off a big event with only a few dollars," Henderson says. She is proud of her staff and describes her relationship with them as "principle-centered" in terms of Steven Covey's leadership strategy. She works hard to apply fairness and equity across the board. "A former worker described me as 'hard but fair.' I can accept that because I am overly work-centered and always up for a good fight on behalf of staff and library needs, even at the risk of being labeled as 'strong-willed.'" Early in her career she found herself in the difficult position of having to fire an employee. "It was by far one of the more difficult things I had done as a young manager at that time," she recounts. "That experience taught me several things about human nature. Since that time I try to maintain an imaginary personal 'do not cross' line and do everything within my purview to ensure the employee knows the expectations of the job and has the opportunity to succeed. However, I impress upon staff that it is up to the individual to avail him- or herself of these opportunities and prove their worth to the organization." Even with her firm work-centered principles, Henderson believes in finding ways to have fun while still being productive. She plays team-building and other asset-development games with the staff, always stressing that there is a lesson to be learned in each game.

As with many in the field, librarianship was not initially a career goal for Henderson. "In college," she says, "I bounced from sociology to political science to nursing—none of which seemed to really fit me. It was only after taking a summer job in a medical library that I decided what career I wanted to pursue. My friends' reactions were obdurate enough when I announced I was pursuing a nursing career, and even worse when I said I was going to become a librarian. My tendency toward fashionable attire was the questioning factor. Friends and associates could not possibly imagine me in any kind of uniform or stereotypical hairdo." However, Henderson had gotten a taste of librarianship and decided to stick with it.

After earning her master's degree from the Graduate School of Library and Information Sciences at the University of Texas at Austin, she had the opportunity to gain work experience in a variety of libraries. Her first directorship was at the St. Paul Medical Center in Dallas, Texas, where she was head of the medical library. "This became my first lead job and proved to be the launching pad of my career as a successful library director," she says. After that first leadership job, she served as executive director of Library Services at Texas Chiropractic College in Pasadena, director of the Georgetown Public Library in Georgetown, and later returned to direct the Pasadena Public Library. Her first public library experience was as library director of the Carol Robert Memorial Library in Brenham. "I perceived this first stint as a public library director to be the greatest fun I had ever experienced," Henderson says. "It was new, different, and challenging. I learned to be very flexible and tolerant of a lot that I would not have accepted in the medical and academic/medical library environment." Later, she applied for the library director position with Pasadena. Her experience and expertise matched the library's needs, and she was hired.

Henderson has many inspiring stories about her experiences as library leader. Two such stories involve children in public libraries. During the summer of her first year in a public library, she encountered many children who tended to roam the library "doing everything except reading." "One child in particular seemed most obnoxious and crude in his remarks and actions," she recalls. She called the boy into her office, chatted with him about his family and his background, and gave him some sports books to read. "I told him he could have them if he agreed to treat them and the staff with respect. He agreed and from that point on I did not have a moment's difficulty with him. I allowed him to get a library card and told him I would be checking his record to see that he did not keep the books past their due dates. He kept his word." Henderson shared this story with the city council during a budget hearing and believes it helped secure funding for a full-time youth position at the library.

"Another incident involved a young girl who had the vocabulary of a foul-mouth whatever!" says Henderson. "She took immense pleasure in visiting the library, harassing other kids, and demonstrating her knowledge of profanity to the staff." The youth and two of her friends were frequently escorted out of the library. Though the library staff had decided it was a lost cause, Henderson decided to write letters to the girls' guardians, explaining their unacceptable behavior and asking permission to meet with the girls and to speak with their school teachers. Permission was granted, and she discovered that the children misbehaved in school as well and were making poor grades. "I met with the girls and outlined library rules, policies, and procedures. I told them I would reward them if they maintained good behavior in the library and at school for three months. Should each be successful, I promised I would take them to Merle Norman Cosmetic Studio for a fashion makeover. That did the trick. Not only did they demonstrate appropriate behavior, their grades improved. At the end of the three months, I took them for the long-awaited visit to the cosmetic studio. Through prearrangement, the owner pampered them and sent them away with a supply of makeup. The girls were so elated with their new look and cosmetics they hastened to share the good news with their friends. They also brought several girls to me who wanted to participate in the same program. This was not exactly what I had signed up for!"

Henderson attributes her success as a leader to a number of factors, among them the guidance and training she has received throughout her lifetime. "I subscribe to the theory that to be a good leader, you must have first been a good follower," she says. "Through the years, I have learned to listen beyond a person's words to hear what is actually being conveyed. That process involves reviewing their past and present history as well as their perception of where they may be headed and what it will require of them to get there. This helps in determining abilities and limitations of staff. Helping staff to identify their strengths and assisting them in planning how to use these strengths for both personal and professional benefit is credited as a major part of my success as a leader." Henderson also believes that her determination to find solutions to problems, her drive to reach goals, and her adeptness at conserving resources and at completing tasks in a timely manner have all been factors attributing to her professional achievements.

"The best role I play is being myself," says Henderson. "I am a people person and every encounter with individuals or groups is an opportunity to share a piece of the library world. I try to take advantage of those moments. My son respectfully suggests that I do not know how to 'turn work off.'"

Henderson is an active member of a number of professional organizations, including American Library Association, Public Library Association, Texas Library Association, and TMLDA. She has served on many committees within these organizations. "Participating and sharing in professional environments offers many opportunities for growth and development that one cannot hope to acquire sitting in an office," she says. "Belonging is not good enough. One has to participate to give and receive the best of what there is in our profession. The skills and information learned through active participation are guaranteed to make a difference in one's attitude toward work."

Henderson believes that the job market demands people with good leadership skills. "If one wants to become a respected and well-developed director," she says, "it is essential to plan the course." She recommends taking courses on library administration and management, information management, information networking, information dissemination and retrieval, and information storage. She is also a big believer in programmed leadership courses such as the "Steven Covey 7 Habits Course." Finally, she advises the development of good communication skills, an understanding of diversity, the ability to manage change, and the use of lateral thinking in problem solving.

"The librarian today has many challenges—more specifically long-standing stereotypes—to overcome," says Henderson. "No longer is it enough to be looked at as the good and passionate librarian or the avid reader. For far too long the profession has suffered from the image of buns, glasses, and orthopedic shoes. Because librarians are finally gaining recognition for their diverse abilities and skills, we must now find a way to turn our challenges into opportunities. Collaborations are encouraged and rewarded in the form of huge grants. Public librarians must match their assets with the needs of the community and build partnerships. The government is putting more money into head-start programs. Here is an opportunity on which we can capitalize. 'Seize the opportunity' must become second nature for us, and publicizing the benefit of that opportunity is a major part of our responsibility as library leaders. 'Marketing' is no longer a concept to be minimized in its impact on helping libraries improve their images and in attracting traditional users as well as a whole host of nontraditional users. In this new millennium, it is essential that the librarian be prepared to step up to the plate."

Wayne J. Peay

WAYNE J. PEAY
Director
Spencer S. Eccles Health Sciences Library
University of Utah
Salt Lake City, Utah

"I would hope that every librarian would, at some point in [his or her] career, consider becoming a library director." Early in his career as a librarian, Wayne Peay did more than consider the idea; he made it his goal. With some years of experience under his belt and a little bit of luck, he achieved his goal in short order.

As director of the Spencer S. Eccles Health Sciences Library at University of Utah, Peay's many responsibilities fall within two categories: external and internal. Externally, Peay represents the library and protects its interests at various meetings, focusing on collaboration, communication, and coordination as essential strategies for success. "Inside the library," he says, "the director's responsibility is to assemble the larger vision and secure the resources to make that vision possible." He constantly strives to bring together the various perspectives of his entire staff, which consists of thirteen librarians, twenty-one support staff members, and eighteen hourly assistants.

Good ideas are encouraged in Peay's library rather than stifled by concerns about funding. "Funding is the director's job," he says. "In no small way, this job is all about sales. I have to communicate the value of our library to secure the resources we need and to develop the internal and external support necessary for high-quality work." Not surprisingly, Peay finds this to be the most difficult aspect of his job. "Every possible source is exploited to provide funding for our library—institutional funds, generated income, grants, contracts, and gifts. Each of these sources has its own requirements and too often we end up getting our financial education in the school of hard knocks."

The Spencer S. Eccles Library is a health sciences library and serves practitioners, researchers, and students involved in the health professions. "Many of our patrons have or are pursuing advanced degrees and have very high expectations," says Peay. "This is a community that understands the importance of information, which is crucial in high-quality education and research programs. For clinical care, information can truly influence patient care."

Within the large and diverse information community, Peay's role is that of leadership. "An academic health sciences library is in a nice position to provide leadership in the development and application of advanced information technologies and services," he explains. "We are not too big or too small. We have access to and are expected to pursue grant funding. Fortunately, the National Library of Medicine supports innovation through its extramural funding program. For the technology and communications components of the information community, we certainly encourage innovation but, equally important, we are advocates for the communities we serve."

"The most challenging aspect of the work is looking over the horizon," Peay continues. "In this rapidly changing environment, a library's best strategy is to be at least slightly ahead of the curve. Innovation is the key component of our library's mission statement and our responsibility as an academic health sciences library."

As an undergraduate, Peay sampled a variety of disciplines. "Like many in our profession, I am an accidental librarian," he says. "I started in engineering, moved into anthropology and geology, spent some time in English, and then got my bachelor's degree in history from the University of Utah. While eight years for a bachelor's degree is not terribly efficient, this survey of various disciplines actually proved to be valuable as my career developed."

Librarianship got into his blood when, still an undergraduate, he was hired as the bindery clerk at the Spencer S. Eccles Health Sciences Library. When he moved into the position of serials assistant, he gained valuable experience working with PHILSOM, one of the first library networks to take on the challenge of serials management. "While there were nights when I dreamed of cascades of punch cards and times when I thought I might blow up that distant computer, it was a great opportunity to learn," Peay says. "The computer had strengths and weaknesses, but what was really powerful were the seven network libraries working collaboratively to solve shared problems."

When he completed his undergraduate degree, Peay was hired as director of the PHILSOM network and serials librarian at the Washington University School of Medicine Library. While there, he found a mentor in Estelle Broadman. "Dr. Broadman was far more interested in her library as a laboratory than in the basic issues of library operations," he says. "She had the highest expectations of everyone in her library, a standard she applied equally to herself. It was an extraordinary experience and directly led to a career in health sciences libraries. After two years, I realized I wanted to pursue a career in libraries and would need a library degree. I also knew that I wanted to be a library director."

Peay attended the School of Library Service at Columbia University in New York. While in library school, he worked at the Medical Library Center of New York. "Working and going to library school in New York City was terrific," he says. "No environment could offer a greater diversity of libraries." After graduating, he moved back to Utah and into the position of media services librarian at the Spencer S. Eccles Health Sciences Library. Knowing that moving up to a director's position would probably require taking a position in another library, he didn't expect to stay at the Eccles library for long. However, the person who was director at the time soon announced her retirement. "At that time I was head of the Computer and Media Services department. I applied for the director position and knew it was a long reach, since I had not been a deputy or associate director. I was also an internal candidate, which is very difficult since you are always surrounded by the process. After what seemed like an endless review of possible candidates, I was selected for the position and officially appointed."

Soon after becoming director, Peay found himself in conflict with a dean at the health sciences center. The disagreement could easily have cost him his dream job, but was nevertheless an eye-opening experience. "In a meeting with the dean, it was explained to me that while I didn't report to him he could have me fired," he recounts. "As the meeting progressed, it was apparent that this was mostly about power. He was a dean and I was only a library director. It quickly became clear that for me to be effective as the library director I had to be prepared to walk away from the job that I worked hard to get. Finally, I explained to the dean that even though I didn't directly report to him, I had to have his confidence, and if I didn't, my resignation was on the table. While the experience was stressful, it actually was, in a sense, liberating. To take the risks that need to be taken, you need to be able to lose."

To Peay, keeping up with technology is not only essential, it is also a fun aspect of his job. He reads eight to ten professional journals regularly and follows half a dozen technology trade publications. He subscribes to several electronic news summaries and reads the technology section of the *New York Times*. In addition, he maintains contacts with colleagues in the larger computing and networking community and takes advantage of lecture opportunities offered at the university.

Peay is a big advocate for membership in professional associations. "They are a primary source for training and continuing education," he says. "Equally important, they are the principal venue for developing the personal networks that are both crucial and one of the great benefits of membership in a profession." He is an active member of a number of professional organizations, most notably the Medical Library Association (MLA). He has served on a variety of MLA committees and sections, including the Copyright Committee, Program Committee, Medical School Libraries Section, Medical Informatics Section, Nominating Committee, and the board of directors. "The Medical Library Association has the broadest membership. It offers both national and regional programs and many opportunities to participate on committees and in sections. In addition to the education programs, direct participation offers opportunities to polish communication skills."

Peay has authored more than fifteen research articles and publications and has given more than forty presentations at national and regional professional conferences. He has been the principal investigator for numerous grant projects and has served as a consultant for various programs at institutions nationwide. In addition, he has been the recipient of a number of honors and awards throughout his career.

Being very content with his job, Peay would like to encourage others to consider becoming library directors. "I have met many talented librarians who simply have never thought about becoming a director," he says. "There is no one, best path to becoming a director. However, a great strategy is to talk with a library director." He also encourages students to take management classes and courses in research methods in library school and elsewhere. Experience with financing and budgeting is also important, and Peay recommends gaining experience with spreadsheets, accounting, and financial planning.

"In academic libraries, the teaching, research, and service expectation is very real," he continues. "Librarians excel in service and increasingly in teaching. The research aspects—grants and publications—are more difficult but are often the deciding factor in the selection process. Building a strong curriculum vitae (CV) is a fundamental strategy in higher education and is an essential requirement in becoming a director. Directors are selected by faculty, and the CV is the traditional measure of faculty excellence." In the CV, Peay recommends including job experience, participation in professional organizations, authored publications, presentations given, and funded grants.

"The opportunities for becoming a director are rapidly increasing," Peay says. "My generation of library directors will pass from the scene during the next ten years. This will result in more than half of the director positions being vacated during this next decade. I believe that with a well-developed career plan and a little luck, a new library school graduate could become director in as little as seven years."

"This is a great—and important—time to be a librarian," he continues. "We are in the midst of a revolution. Exciting new technologies are emerging that will be just as important to us as books have been in the past. Access to new knowledge could truly be transformational but the outcome of this revolution is very uncertain. However, librarians are truly in the position to shape this outcome and assure an exciting future."

For more information about Wayne Peay, you may find his CV on the Spencer S. Eccles Library website at http://medlib.med.utah.edu.

MARY KATHLEEN PRICE
Director of the Law Library
and Professor of Law
New York University Law Library
New York, N.Y.

Mary Kathleen Price

If a background rich in knowledge and experience is one of the keys to successful library directorship, Kathleen Price is well suited for the job. At New York University School of Law, she serves as director of the law library and professor of law. Before accepting her current position, however, she set about gathering under her belt a variety of professional experiences in two seemingly disparate fields—law and librarianship. Her successes prove that the two disciplines can be gainfully merged.

The idea of becoming a law librarian first took root when Price was an undergraduate on a state teaching scholarship at the University of Florida (UF). "I read an article in the school newspaper about Betty Taylor, the law librarian at UF, who had worked her way through law school a course at a time while working in the library," Price explains. "Knowing that I wanted to attend law school, I tucked away that information until later." After graduating with her B.A. in political science, she enrolled in the library science program at Florida State University and completed her master's degree in library science on an Office of Education fellowship.

After library school, Price accepted a position as a cataloger at the University of Alabama Law Library, where she had the opportunity to study law on a part-time basis. After taking three years to complete her first year of J.D. course work, she moved on to complete her law degree at the University of Illinois, where she simultaneously served as associate librarian. "I then practiced for two years as a litigator with the liberal

Democratic firm of Ross, Hardies, O'Keefe, Babcock, and Parsons in Chicago, founded by robber baron Samuel Insull as the 'blue-collar boys' to represent the gas company," says Price. The only woman on the firm at the time, she worked primarily on explosion cases and construction litigation.

During her second year at the firm, Price was approached by Duke University and asked to become its law librarian. Having always been interested in a career as a legal educator, she accepted the position. "At Duke I was influenced by Dean Kenneth Pye to teach substantive criminal law, to be an active participant in the life of the law school, and to join the faculty twice a day for coffee to keep up with their research," she says. This advice served her well throughout her career at Duke and later at University of Minnesota, where she served as director of the law library and briefly as acting assistant vice president for Academic Affairs. At Minnesota she taught criminal law, torts, and biomedical ethics and twice served as exchange professor to Uppsala University in Sweden.

"Minnesota was my entrée to foreign and international educational issues that altered the course of my career," Price says. A month after her arrival she was appointed a member of University of Minnesota's first faculty delegation to China. "Not only did I become connected to the most influential faculty but I also began a relationship with Chinese law schools that has already lasted twenty-three years!" As the librarian board member of the Ford Foundation–funded Committee on Legal Education with China, Price oversaw a program to rebuild law libraries in seven prestigious law schools, placed librarians from each school in American library schools, coordinated continuing education seminars in China for law librarians, organized book donation programs, and fostered electronic research programs.

In 1990, Price added "Law Librarian of Congress" to her already impressive CV. As the person responsible for the world's largest law library, her most visible duty was to serve as research director for thirty foreign legal specialists providing foreign, comparative, and international law research to Congress and providing opinions to the Immigration and Naturalization Service on country conditions. Due to budget constraints, political instability, and difficulties working with the foreign legal specialists, the job was a stressful one for Price. "I had no notion of the difficulties in being a change agent in an underfunded, underappreciated service unit," she says.

Always interested in global law, Price accepted her current position at New York University (NYU) law school mainly because it proclaimed itself to be the first global law school. "Here we attempt to support the country's most distinguished international law faculty, 400 foreign graduate law students, and an increasingly internationally focused J.D. student body in an increasingly electronic environment," she says. "I love the intellectual stimulation of NYU and the creativity in providing service to a demanding but appreciative clientele."

"Due to our creative, committed library faculty, we have been able to accomplish a great deal at NYU despite a flat budget and a staff too small for a multidivisional program," says Price. Her library proved itself to be a "law library pioneer in digitization" through participation in a legal history project involving nineteenth-century family law. In addition, Price has been the principal investigator in a research project to build an electronic law library partnership to offer 24/7 reference support to patrons of nine participating law libraries located approximately six hours apart around the globe. "If I have made a contribution to law librarianship," she says, "it is in the area of creating international partnerships."

Price perceives her role to be that of "cheerleader, grant getter, and 'grande dame' of law librarianship." Her leadership style is best described as "walk around": "I have tea every day at three with technical services, for example," she explains. "I confer daily with the associate librarians but trust them to supervise their staffs. My mentor Ken Pye operated on the principle that one should hire staff smarter than oneself, delegate to them, and reap the praise for their performance! I care about results but don't micromanage."

Throughout her career, Price has conducted research and written numerous papers on topics such as access to legal information, foreign and international law, intellectual property, and digitization standards. She takes courses and attends workshops regularly. She has been past-president of the American Association of Law Libraries and maintains an active membership in that organization as well as other national and international law and library associations.

"The combination of law and librarianship has made me a strong articulator," says Price. Being open and extroverted has helped her to achieve success throughout her career. She advises would-be law library directors to teach and write. "Now is the time for bright, multilingual, law-trained librarians to enter the job market," she says. "We face losing up to half of our sitting directors in the next five to ten years. Because law library directors have moved away from teaching substantive law, they are being replaced by administrators without faculty status and tenure."

Price feels that today's librarians don't receive the respect they deserve. "When I entered the profession in 1967, a recent poll found librarianship to be in the top five least stressful professions," she says. "Today, the demands upon us and the uncertainties in the arena in which we work make librarianship among the most stressful. We get little respect or financial reward for making our patrons look brilliant. We need to realize and fight for respect for information professionals in an information age!"

Dale Canelas
Courtesy of Randy Batista/
Media Image Photography

DALE CANELAS
Director of Libraries
University of Florida
George A. Smathers Libraries
Gainesville, Fla.

"Like many librarians, I came to librarianship late," says Dale Canelas. "I didn't know about the field as a student, there were no family members or friends who were librarians, and I was in my mid-twenties before I read about the profession and began to understand that it suited my talents." Today, as director of libraries at the University of Florida, Canelas is responsible for representing the interests of eight campus libraries known as the George A. Smathers Libraries. Together these libraries employ 95 professionals, 165 support staff, and 75 FTE student assistants. Though she says that early in her career she did not know that she might wish to become a director, Canelas has now realized her full potential in the ultimate position of library directorship.

As the largest library system in Florida, the Smathers Libraries play an active role in national research library initiatives and cooperative programs, and in resource sharing on the local and national level. "Locally, library staff are deeply involved in integrating new technologies and formats with traditional collections and information sources," Canelas says. "We were the first in the country to use e-mail for reference questions, the first university to sign a contract with Elsevier, and were early adopters of online processes for student/faculty off-site use of ILL and circulation services." In addition, the reference department was one of the first to implement chat reference. Clearly, during the last two decades the Smathers Libraries have been pioneers in the incorporation of electronic technology in library services.

"As director of university libraries I report to the provost, represent the university in national, regional, and statewide library organizations, and oversee the tenure and promotion process for all librarians regardless of location," says Canelas. "My role encompasses both external and internal relationships. Keeping up with national library developments, evaluating what the university needs in terms of library service, working with directors and department chairs to develop library programs, and marshalling the library's resources (both human and monetary) to provide the required services keep me pretty busy. I attend many university meetings where the university's direction and priorities are discussed, and I share this information with associate directors and department chairs so that we can work together in identifying how the library will support their initiatives." Canelas also spends time representing the university library system at professional meetings of information technology organizations such as the Association of Research Libraries (ARL). She encourages library staff to attend such meetings when appropriate, both to share experiences with others and to bring back relevant ideas that might enrich the organization.

"Like most ARL library directors, my schedule is variable depending upon the time of year and the library's current initiatives," says Canelas. "For example, we are now working with architects to design an addition to the main library. I am spending quite a bit of time in meetings with architects, construction firms, and the university's Facilities Planning Office." Fund-raising activities and meetings regarding tenure and promotion consume significant portions of her time as well. In addition, Canelas meets with the people who report to her—four associate directors, the development officer, and the office manager—once each week, and with department chairs and directors once each month. Juggling all of the many conflicting demands of her job is at times difficult, but Canelas realizes that this is part and parcel of a research library director's job.

Canelas finds that the most challenging feature of her job is maintaining high staff morale in the face of frequently variable state resources. "Years of substantial cuts come with some regularity in Florida," she explains. In such situations, the staff is stretched very thinly and changes in a staff member's job parameters are difficult to adjust to. "Occasional huge materials budget windfalls leave selection and acquisitions staff in a paroxysm of purchasing, while receiving and cataloging staff are inundated with materials they can't process. If directors can't predict, with some degree of accuracy, what funding will be available to run the library until after a fiscal year has started, the library's ability to plan its work and communicate objectives to staff is greatly hampered."

Canelas received her bachelor's degree in Spanish language and literature from Loyola University in Chicago. While an undergraduate, she spent a year at the Universidad Nacional Autonoma de Mexico in Mexico City where she studied language, literature, and Latin American history while living with a Mexican family. She returned to the United States fluent in Spanish. Later, she received her master's degree in library science from Dominican University (then Rosary College) in River Forest, Illinois. Early in her career as a librarian, she had the good fortune to work for a young public library director who took the time to explain to Canelas the ins and outs of library directorship. "The year and a half working with him gave me a good sense of what administration is and a well-rounded set of administrative skills for a small organization," she says. "Most important, he taught me what it means to be a professional. When he left the job, he encouraged me to apply for the directorship—an action that required considerable thought on my part because, only two years out of library school, I still thought of myself as a reference librarian and got a lot of satisfaction out of helping people find the information they needed." In the end, Canelas rose to the challenge and decided to apply for library administration positions, changing her focus from public to academic libraries. She began in an administrative position at Northwestern University Library, later moved on to Stanford University and, ultimately, to the University of Florida. "All of my jobs contributed in different ways to developing managerial perspective and skills."

Canelas maintains that librarianship is a graying profession and that the job market in the next ten years should be excellent for those in mid-career who want to become directors. "Good analytic skills are necessary as is treating staff with respect for their professionalism and contributions to the library," she says. "Being able to articulate a library vision and explain the library to nonlibrarians is also important both to obtain resources from the university and to attract donors. A willingness to take reasonable risks is basic to good management and tolerance for change is helpful. Good interpersonal skills are invaluable as is the ability to write cogent and convincing memos. Candidates who can show that they are able to set objectives for themselves and meet them demonstrate directorial potential. Budget experience and the ability to read and understand statistics are very useful. A work history that shows increasing responsibility will speak to a candidate's growth and development—important criteria for a director."

To Canelas, being a librarian today means the same as it always has. "Research libraries have changed diametrically over the past thirty-five years, and yet, they have retained the values of the past—building collections to support the academic programs of the institution, providing access to accumulated knowledge, and training new students in the skills they will need to pursue their educational goals," she explains. "It is true that how we carry out these activities has changed, but the basic activities have not. Whether working with print, microform, or digital collections, we continue to identify with the needs of our university, our students, and our faculty, and to exercise traditional librarian values in providing support for them and for others who come to us for our help."

SAMPLE JOB DESCRIPTION

Library Director

Environment

A library director is responsible for the overall administration and management of a library. In many cases, depending upon the library's size, administrative duties may be shared with an assistant director, an associate director, or a deputy director.

Responsibilities

Establish the library's mission, goals, and objectives and ensure that all library activities support them

Oversee the library's planning processes, including strategic planning and planning for building expansion and renovation

Provide leadership and direction toward the improvement of policies and services as needed

Authorize library policy changes that affect library users

Maintain communication with library users, informing them of the services, policies, and plans of the library and seeking suggestions for possible improvement of services

Prepare the library's annual budget, authorize library expenditures, and supervise financial planning and fund-raising efforts

Supervise and evaluate staff members such as the associate director or the administrative services manager

Oversee and guide the recruitment, selection, and evaluation of library faculty; authorize faculty appointments, salaries, and terminations;

authorize classified personnel appointments, terminations, and future hiring recommendations

Provide direction and guidance to the library's managers in matters relating to personnel, public relations, planning, publicity, reporting, and control

Represent the library's interests to outside organizations

Participate in collaborative endeavors with other libraries and institutions

Participate in library- or institutionwide committees

Maintain a high level of professional competence by keeping abreast of developments in the field

Maintain active memberships in various professional associations

Contribute to the profession of librarianship through service, presentations, or publications

Education and Training

A master's degree in library and information science from an ALA-accredited institution is required. In some cases, an additional advanced degree in another subject area is preferred. Many college and university library director positions require a doctorate. Five to ten years of experience in progressively administrative or supervisory positions are generally required.

Recommended Memberships

PUBLIC LIBRARIES

American Library Association (ALA)

Public Library Association (PLA), a division of ALA

Regional and local library associations

ACADEMIC HEALTH SCIENCES LIBRARIES

Medical Library Association (MLA)

American Medical Informatics Association (AMIA)

National Network of Libraries of Medicine (NN/LM)

Association of Academic Health Sciences Library Directors (AAHSLD)

Regional and local health sciences library associations

UNIVERSITY LIBRARIES

American Library Association (ALA)

Association of Research Libraries (ARL)

Association of College and Research Libraries (ACRL), a division of ALA

Regional and local library associations

LAW LIBRARIES

American Association of Law Libraries (AALL)

Special Libraries Association (SLA)

Regional and local law library associations

Notes

1. Peter Hernon, Ronald R. Powell, and Arthur P. Young, "University Library Directors in the Association of Research Libraries: The Next Generation, Part One," *College and Research Libraries* 62, no. 2 (Mar. 2001): 116–45.

2. Peter McCracken, "The Presence of the Doctorate among Small College Library Directors," *College and Research Libraries* 51, no. 5 (Sept. 2000): 400–8.

LAURA KANE is th   id Acquisitions at
the University of So   hool of Medicine
Library in Columbi   has held this faculty position since g   School of Library
and Information S   is the author of
"Access versus Own   *pedia of Library
and Information S   member of the
Medical Library As   Chapter/Medical
Library Association,   ary Association.